Pat Sloan's

Holiday Hoopla

12 Quilts for Everyday & Special Occasions

Martingale
Create with Confidence

DEDICATION

To my most trusted friend, long-arm quilter, and soul sister, Cindy Dickinson. In 2021 while I was writing this book, Cindy lost her short fierce battle with pancreatic cancer. Cindy has quilted hundreds of my quilts, advised me on designs, laughed and cried with me, and been my buddy for so long, I can't imagine quilting without her to talk to. Please keep her wonderful husband, Dennis, in your thoughts and prayers as he navigates this next chapter in his life without his best friend.

Pat Sloan's Holiday Hoopla: 12 Quilts for Everyday & Special Occasions
© 2022 by Pat Sloan

Martingale®
18939 120th Ave NE, Suite 101
Bothell, WA 98011-9511 USA
ShopMartingale.com

Printed in the United States of America
27 26 25 24 23 22   8 7 6 5 4 3 2 1

Library of Congress Cataloging-in-Publication Data is available upon request.

ISBN: 978-1-68356-219-1

MISSION STATEMENT

We empower makers who use fabric and yarn to make life more enjoyable.

CREDITS

PUBLISHER AND CHIEF VISIONARY OFFICER
Jennifer Erbe Keltner

CONTENT DIRECTOR
Karen Costello Soltys

DESIGN MANAGER
Adrienne Smitke

TECHNICAL EDITOR
Nancy Mahoney

PRODUCTION MANAGER
Regina Girard

COPY EDITOR
Durby Peterson

PHOTOGRAPHER
Brent Kane

ILLUSTRATOR
Sandy Loi

SPECIAL THANKS
Some of the photography for this book was taken at the home of Lianne Anderson in Arlington, Washington.

Contents

Introduction

I'm so excited to welcome you to my tenth book published with Martingale! It's thrilling to be able to work with the best team to bring my ideas to life. *Pat Sloan's Holiday Hoopla* is full of projects you can easily make to decorate for so many different holidays. Some of these ideas I've had for a very long time. It was fun to finally develop them into quilts for you.

We kick off the holidays with A Snow Day on page 7, which isn't an actual holiday on the calendar but is certainly a holiday at my house! Then you'll find 11 more quilts featuring special days you know and love. For your enjoyment, I've also included monthly lists of a few obscure—and maybe a bit nutty—days, such as National Rubber Ducky Day.

I love creating these projects because it makes me happy to switch out a few key pieces to transform the feel in my home. Display one of these quilts, make a few pillows and runners in colors to match, and your rooms can take on a new festive vibe.

One of my favorites is the bookcase quilt on page 69. I still own a few of my first books, thanks to my mom saving them for me! They are truly my treasures. My parents said I was a huge reader; there was always a stack of books waiting to share their stories with me. Books are truly something to be celebrated. You can make the bookcase quilt your own by finding fabric with words that tell a story, and you could even use selvages for the book spines. My shelf is not too neat and tidy—the books are stacked any which way, just like in real life.

Thank you joining me on this holiday hoopla. It's going to be a celebration!

— Pat

Join Me Online

If you follow me online at ILovetoMakeQuilts.com, you can download my monthly calendar, where I list challenges, sew-alongs, and special holidays. I hope you'll join the fun!

A Snow Day

The first snow day of the season is magical! You hope there's enough snow so you can't possibly get out, making it a day to bake cookies, drink hot coffee, and watch big snowflakes fall. Living in New Jersey as a child, I experienced a few big snow days with massive drifts. Later, when I lived in Belgium, we didn't get much snow, so it was spectacular when it did snow!

Materials

Yardage is based on 42"-wide fabric. Fat eighths measure 9" × 21".

- 1⅞ yards of blue dot for background
- ⅞ yard of white print for Pinwheel blocks and Snowman
- 1 fat eighth of black dot for Snowman hat
- 2 fat eighths of coral prints for scarf
- 5" × 7" piece of charcoal print for eyes and buttons
- ⅜ yard of black diagonal stripe for binding
- 2½ yards of fabric for backing
- 45" × 54" piece of batting

Cutting

All measurements include ¼" seam allowances. As you cut, label the pieces as indicated for easy assembly.

From the blue dot, cut:
1 strip, 10½" × 42"; crosscut into:
    1 piece, 7" × 10½" (X)
    1 piece, 5½" × 10½" (Y)
    1 piece, 5" × 10½" (Z)
    1 piece, 4" × 10½" (W)
1 strip, 9½" × 42"; crosscut into:
    1 piece, 8¾" × 9½" (Q)
    1 piece, 5½" × 9½" (S)
    1 strip, 3" × 9½" (EE)
    1 strip, 2½" × 9½" (DD)

Continued on page 8

January 3: *International Mind-Body Wellness Day*

January 4: *National Spaghetti Day*

January 10: *National Houseplant Appreciation Day*

January 13: *National Rubber Ducky Day*

January 25: *Opposite Day*

Continued from page 7

From the blue dot, cut:

1 strip, 6" × 42"; crosscut into:
- 1 piece, 6" × 8½" (N)
- 1 piece, 5½" × 8½" (K)
- 1 piece, 4½" × 8¾" (E)
- 2 squares, 3½" × 3½" (FF)

1 strip, 3¼" × 42"; crosscut into:
- 1 piece, 3¼" × 9¾" (J)
- 1 piece, 3¼" × 7¼" (I)
- 1 piece, 3" × 8¾" (F)

6 strips, 2½" × 42"; crosscut into:
- 1 strip, 2½" × 11½" (U)
- 20 pieces, 2½" × 4½" (B)
- 48 squares, 2½" × 2½" (A)

4 strips, 2" × 42"; crosscut into:
- 1 strip, 2" × 17½" (GG)
- 1 strip, 2" × 16¾" (G)
- 1 strip, 2" × 13½" (L)
- 2 strips, 2" × 8½" (T)
- 1 strip, 2" × 6½" (CC)
- 5 strips, 2" × 6" (D)
- 1 strip, 2" × 5" (AA)
- 5 pieces, 2" × 3½" (V)
- 1 piece, 2" × 2½" (R)
- 3 squares, 2" × 2" (BB)

3 strips, 1¾" × 42"; crosscut into:
- 1 strip, 1¾" × 39" (M)
- 1 strip, 1¾" × 30" (II)
- 2 strips, 1¾" × 5¾" (H)
- 1 piece, 1¾" × 2" (C)

2 strips, 1½" × 42"; crosscut into:
- 1 strip, 1½" × 18½" (HH)
- 1 strip, 1½" × 14" (O)
- 1 strip, 1½" × 8½" (P)

From the white print, cut:

1 strip, 10" × 42"; crosscut into:
- 1 piece, 10" × 18½" (O)
- 1 strip, 5" × 18½" (N)

1 strip, 4½" × 42"; crosscut into:
- 1 strip, 4½" × 11½" (K)
- 1 strip, 4" × 11½" (L)
- 1 strip, 3" × 12½" (E)
- 1 strip, 1" × 12½" (F)

3 strips, 2½" × 42"; crosscut into:
- 1 strip, 2½" × 9½" (H)
- 20 pieces, 2½" × 4½" (A)

3 strips, 2" × 42"; crosscut into:
- 1 strip, 2" × 12½" (G)
- 4 strips, 2" × 8¾" (M)
- 1 strip, 2" × 7¾" (J)
- 2 strips, 2" × 5¾" (D)
- 3 pieces, 2" × 3½" (C)
- 1 piece, 2" × 2¾" (I)
- 5 squares, 2" × 2" (B)

From the black dot, cut:

1 piece, 4½" × 5¾" (A)

1 strip, 2" × 7" (B)

From *each* of the coral prints, cut:

2 strips, 2" × 21"; crosscut into
- 13 squares, 2" × 2" (26 total)

From the charcoal print, cut:

6 squares, 2" × 2"

From the black diagonal stripe, cut:

5 strips, 2¼" × 42"

Making the Pinwheel Blocks

Press seam allowances in the directions indicated by the arrows.

1 Draw a diagonal line from corner to corner on the wrong side of 40 blue A squares. Place a marked square on one end of a white A, right sides together. Sew on the marked line. Trim the excess corner fabric ¼" from the stitched line. Place a marked blue square on the opposite end of the white piece. Sew and trim as before to make a flying-geese unit measuring 2½" × 4½", including seam allowances. Make 20 units.

Make 20 units,
2½" × 4½".

2 Join a blue B and a flying-geese unit as shown. Make 20 units measuring 4½" square, including seam allowances.

Make 20 units,
4½" × 4½".

Keeping Track

With so many different square and strip sizes cut from each fabric, it pays to label your pieces with their corresponding letter so you can see at a glance which pieces you need for each unit. Use sticky notes, lettered pins, zip-top bags, or whatever works best for you.

3 Lay out four units from step 2 in two rows of two, rotating the units to make a pinwheel. Sew the units into rows and then join the rows. Make five Pinwheel blocks measuring 8½" square, including seam allowances.

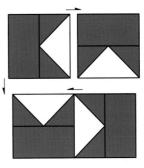

Make 5 blocks,
8½" × 8½".

Making the Top Section

1 Join blue D and C pieces to a white B square. Add the blue E and blue F pieces. Sew a Pinwheel block to the right edge of the unit and the blue G strip to the bottom to make a left unit measuring 10" × 16¾", including seam allowances.

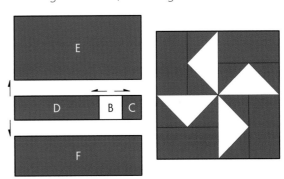

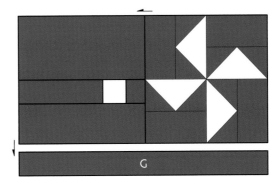

Make 1 left unit,
10" × 16¾".

2 Join the two blue H strips to the black A piece. Sew the black B to the bottom and the blue I to the right edge of the unit. Sew the blue J to the top of the unit to make a center unit measuring 9¾" × 10", including seam allowances.

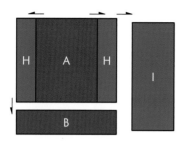

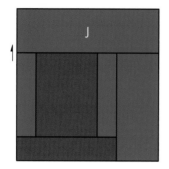

Make 1 center unit,
9¾" × 10".

3 Join a Pinwheel block and the blue K piece. Sew the blue L strip to the top to make a right unit measuring 10" × 13½", including seam allowances.

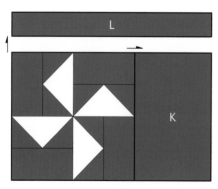

Make 1 right unit,
10" × 13½".

4 Join the units from steps 1–3. Sew the blue M strip to the top edge. The top section should measure 11¼" × 39", including seam allowances.

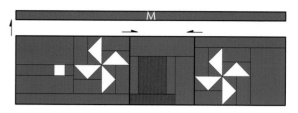

Make 1 top section,
11¼" × 39".

Making the Left Section

1 Sew the blue N piece to the bottom of a Pinwheel block. Sew the blue O strip to the left edge to make a unit measuring 9½" × 14", including seam allowances.

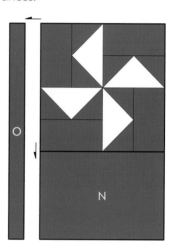

Make 1 unit,
9½" × 14".

2 Sew the blue P strip to the right edge of a Pinwheel block to make a unit measuring 8½" × 9½", including seam allowances.

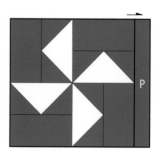

Make 1 unit,
8½" × 9½".

Pat Sloan's Holiday Hoopla

3 Join the blue R and D pieces and a white B square. Add the blue Q and S pieces to make a unit measuring 9½" × 15¼", including seam allowances.

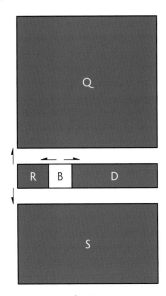

Make 1 unit,
9½" × 15¼".

4 Join the units from steps 1–3 to make the left section, which should measure 9½" × 36¾", including seam allowances.

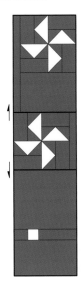

Make 1 left section,
9½" × 36¾".

Making the Right Section

1 Sew blue T strips to the top and bottom of a Pinwheel block. Add the blue U strip to make a unit measuring 10½" × 11½", including seam allowances.

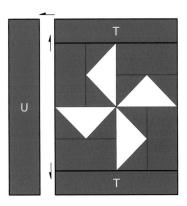

Make 1 unit,
10½" × 11½".

2 Join blue V and D pieces to a white B square. Repeat to make three units measuring 2" × 10½", including seam allowances.

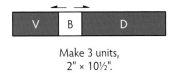

Make 3 units,
2" × 10½".

3 Join the blue W, X, Y and Z pieces and the units from steps 1 and 2 as shown to make the right section, which should measure 10½" × 35½", including seam allowances. Note that one of the rows from step 2 is rotated 180°.

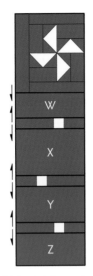

Make 1 right section,
10½" × 35½".

Making the Snowman

The snowman is made from two pieced units—the head and the body.

HEAD UNIT

1 Join two different coral squares to make a two-patch. Make 13 units measuring 2" × 3½", including seam allowances.

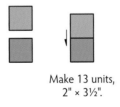

Make 13 units,
2" × 3½".

2 Lay out two blue V, one blue AA, one blue BB, one blue CC pieces, and three two-patch units as shown. Sew all the pieces into columns and then join the columns to make a unit measuring 5" × 9½", including seam allowances.

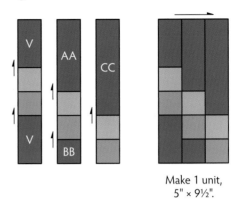

Make 1 unit,
5" × 9½".

3 Join three white C and two charcoal squares. Join two white D and one charcoal square. Join the rows and white E, F, and G strips to make a unit measuring 8" × 12½", including seam allowances.

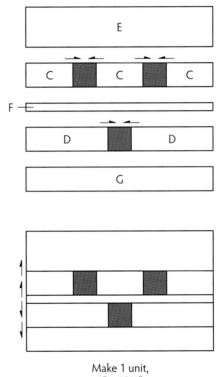

Make 1 unit,
8" × 12½".

4 Draw a diagonal line from corner to corner on the wrong side of two blue A and two blue BB squares. Place marked A squares on the upper-left and upper-right corners of the unit from step 3, right sides together. Place marked BB squares on the lower-left and lower-right corners of the unit. Sew on the marked lines. Trim the excess corner fabric ¼" from the stitched lines. The unit should measure 8" × 12½", including seam allowances.

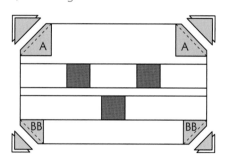

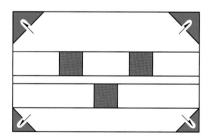

Make 1 unit,
8" × 12½".

5 Join four coral two-patch units end to end to make a row. Sew the row to the bottom of the unit from step 4 to make a unit measuring 9½" × 12½", including seam allowances.

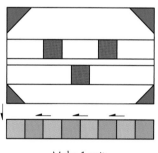

Make 1 unit,
9½" × 12½".

6 Sew the unit from step 2 to the left edge of the unit from step 5. Sew the blue DD strip to the right edge of the unit. The head unit should measure 9½" × 19", including seam allowances.

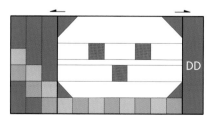

Make 1 unit,
9½" × 19".

BODY UNIT

1 Draw a diagonal line from corner to corner on the wrong side of six blue A squares. Place a marked A square on each end of the white H strip, right sides together. Sew on the marked lines. Trim the excess corner fabric ¼" from the stitched lines. The unit should measure 2½" × 9½", including seam allowances.

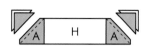

Make 1 unit,
2½" × 9½".

2 Join six coral two-patch units from step 1 of "Head Unit" on page 12 to make a unit measuring 3½" × 9½", including seam allowances.

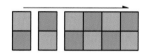

Make 1 unit,
3½" × 9½".

3 Join the white I, one charcoal square, and the white J. Sew a white K and L to the top and bottom edges. The unit should measure 9½" × 11½", including seam allowances.

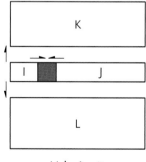

Make 1 unit,
9½" × 11½".

4 Place marked A squares from step 1 on the upper-right and lower-right corners of the unit from step 3. Sew on the marked lines. Trim the excess corner fabric ¼" from the stitched lines. The unit should measure 9½" × 11½", including seam allowances.

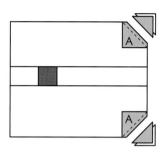

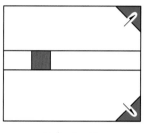

Make 1 unit,
9½" × 11½".

5 Join the blue EE strip and the units from steps 1, 2, and 4 as shown to make the upper-body unit, which should measure 9½" × 19", including seam allowances.

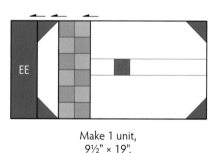

Make 1 unit,
9½" × 19".

6 Join two white M pieces and one charcoal square. Make two units measuring 2" × 18½", including seam allowances.

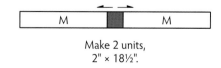

Make 2 units,
2" × 18½".

A Snow Day

7 Join the two units from step 6 with the white N and O pieces to make a unit measuring 17½" × 18½", including seam allowances.

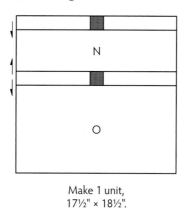

Make 1 unit,
17½" × 18½".

8 Draw a diagonal line from corner to corner on the wrong side of the blue FF squares. Place marked FF squares on the upper-left and upper-right corners of the unit from step 7. Sew on the marked lines. Trim the excess corner fabric ¼" from the stitched lines. Place marked A squares from step 1 on the lower-left and lower-right corners of the unit. Sew and trim as before to make a unit measuring 17½" × 18½", including seam allowances.

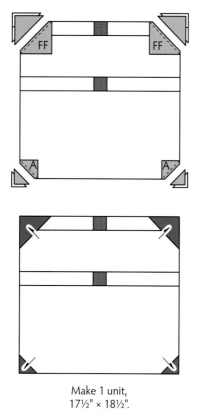

Make 1 unit,
17½" × 18½".

9 Sew the blue GG strip to the left edge of the unit from step 8 to make the lower-body unit, which should measure 17½" × 20", including seam allowances.

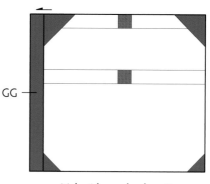

Make 1 lower-body unit,
17½" × 20".

Assembling the Quilt Top

1 Join the head and upper-body units. Sew the blue HH strip to the right edge and then add the lower-body unit to make the snowman section, which should measure 20" × 35½", including seam allowances.

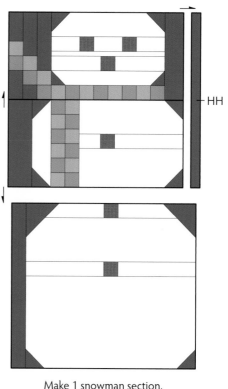

Make 1 snowman section,
20" × 35½".

2 Referring to the quilt assembly diagram below, sew the right section to the snowman. Sew the blue II strip to the bottom edge. Sew the left section to the snowman and add the top section. The quilt top should measure 39" × 47½".

Finishing the Quilt

For more details on any finishing steps, visit ShopMartingale.com/HowtoQuilt for free downloadable information.

1 Layer the quilt top with batting and backing; baste the layers together.

2 Quilt by hand or machine. The quilt shown is machine quilted with a snowflake design in the Pinwheel blocks. A small meandering design is stitched in the snowman, and a large meandering design is stitched in the background.

3 Use the black stripe 2¼"-wide strips to make double-fold binding. Attach the binding to the quilt.

Quilt assembly

Key to My Heart

FINISHED QUILT: 26½" × 38½" • **FINISHED BLOCKS: 6" × 6" and 6" × 7"**

I've combined two loves—keys and hearts—to celebrate one of my favorite months, February! Hearts have been my "thing" for as long as I can remember—I put **XOXO** and little hearts on everything. As for keys, my grandfather made keys for people and had a huge box of old-fashioned keys in his attic. I loved playing with them. His home also had a wonderful skeleton key for the front door, so I have such great memories whenever I see a key like that.

Materials

Yardage is based on 42"-wide fabric. Fat eighths measure 9" × 21".

- 1 yard of white print for background and border
- 5" × 12" piece of red dot for Heart blocks
- 1 fat eighth of pink plaid for Heart blocks and border
- ⅝ yard of red dot for key section and binding
- 2 squares, 8" × 8" *each*, of red prints for letter blocks
- 2 pieces, 5" × 14" *each*, of pink prints for letter blocks
- 1¼ yards of fabric for backing
- 33" × 45" piece of batting

Cutting

All measurements include ¼" seam allowances. As you cut, label the pieces as indicated for easy assembly.

From the white print, cut:
1 strip, 6" × 42"; crosscut into 1 strip, 6" × 24½" (E)
1 strip, 4½" × 42"; crosscut into:
    1 strip, 4½" × 14" (F)
    1 square, 4½" × 4½" (K)
    2 squares, 4" × 4" (A)
1 strip, 3½" × 42"; crosscut into:
    3 squares, 3½" × 3½" (N)
    4 squares, 3" × 3" (C)
    2 squares, 2¾" × 2¾" (O)

Continued on page 20

Fun Days to Celebrate in February

February 4: *National Homemade Soup Day*

February 7: *National Periodic Table Day*

February 11: *National Make a Friend Day*

February 20: *National Cherry Pie Day*

February 26: *National Letter to an Elder Day*

Continued from page 19

From the white print, cut:

5 strips, 2½" × 42"; crosscut into:

    3 strips, 2½" × 34½" (R)

    2 strips, 2½" × 22½" (S)

    2 strips, 2½" × 6½" (D)

    1 piece, 2½" × 4½" (I)

    2 squares, 2½" × 2½" (M)

2 strips, 2" × 42"; crosscut into:

    1 strip, 2" × 17¼" (H)

    1 strip, 2" × 5¾" (J)

    8 squares, 2" × 2" (B)

    2 strips, 1¾" × 4½" (G)

    1 piece, 1¾" × 2" (Q)

1 strip, 1½" × 42"; crosscut into:

    4 strips, 1½" × 6½" (L)

    2 strips, 1½" × 4½" (P)

From the red dot for Heart block, cut:

1 square, 4" × 4" (A)

2 squares, 3½" × 3½" (T)

From the pink plaid for Heart block, cut:

1 square, 4" × 4" (A)

2 squares, 3½" × 3½" (T)

2 squares, 3" × 3" (C)

From the red dot for key section, cut:

1 strip, 3½" × 42"; crosscut into:

    1 strip, 3½" × 24½" (U)

    2 squares, 3" × 3" (C)

2 strips, 2½" × 42"; crosscut into:

    2 strips, 2½" × 10½" (V)

    2 strips, 2½" × 6½" (D)

    1 strip, 2½" × 6" (W)

    2 strips, 2½" × 4½" (X)

4 strips, 2¼" × 42"

From *1* red square, cut:

1 piece, 2½" × 6½" (J)

1 piece, 2½" × 4½" (I)

From *1* red square, cut:

2 pieces, 3½" × 6½" (Y)

From *1* pink square, cut:

4 pieces, 2" × 3½" (Z)

2 squares, 2½" × 2½" (M)

From *1* pink square, cut:

1 strip, 2½" × 6½" (D)

2 strips, 1¾" × 4½" (G)

1 piece, 2" × 3¼" (AA)

Making the Heart Blocks

Press seam allowances in the directions indicated by the arrows.

1 Draw a diagonal line from corner to corner on the wrong side of the white A squares. Layer a marked square on a red A, right sides together. Sew ¼" from both sides of the drawn line. Cut the unit apart on the marked line. Make two half-square-triangle units and trim them to 3½" square, including seam allowances. Repeat using the remaining marked square and the pink A to make two units.

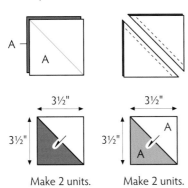

Make 2 units.   Make 2 units.

2 Draw a diagonal line from corner to corner on the wrong side of the white B squares. Place a marked square on one corner of a red T. Sew on the marked line. Trim the excess corner fabric ¼" from the stitched line. Place a marked square on an adjacent corner of the square. Sew and trim as before. Make two units measuring 3½" square, including seam allowances. Repeat using the remaining marked squares and the pink T to make two units.

Make 2 of each unit,
3½" × 3½".

3 Lay out one red and one pink unit each from steps 1 and 2 in two rows as shown. Sew the units into rows and then join the rows. Make one Heart block measuring 6½" square, including seam allowances. Repeat to make a mirror-image block.

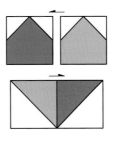 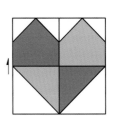

Make 1 block,
6½" × 6½".

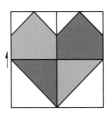

Make 1 block,
6½" × 6½".

Making the Key Section

1 Sew a white D strip to the left and right sides of the mirror-image Heart block to make a unit measuring 6½" × 10½".

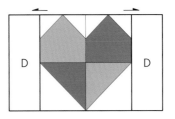

Make 1 unit,
6½" × 10½".

2 Draw a diagonal line from corner to corner on the wrong side of two white C squares. Layer a marked square on a red C square, right sides together. Sew ¼" from both sides of the drawn line. Cut the

unit apart on the marked line. Make four half-square-triangle units and trim them to 2½" square, including seam allowances.

Make 4 units.

3 Sew a red D strip to the left and right sides of the unit from step 1. Sew the triangle units from step 2 to the ends of the red V strips. Sew these units to the top and bottom to make the key top, which should measure 10½" × 14½", including seam allowances.

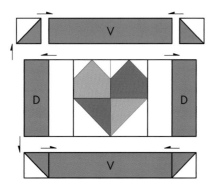

Make 1 key top, 10½" × 14½".

4 Join the white E and red U to make a unit measuring 9" × 24½", including seam allowances.

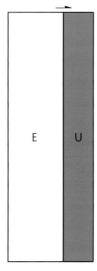

Make 1 unit, 9" × 24½".

5 Join one white G and one red X. Sew the white F to the red strip. Sew a white H strip to the right edge to make a unit measuring 6" × 17¼", including seam allowances.

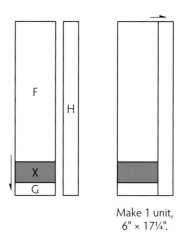

Make 1 unit, 6" × 17¼".

6 Join one white G and one red X. Sew the white I to the red strip. Sew a white J strip to the right side. Sew a red W strip to the top to make a unit measuring 6" × 7¾", including seam allowances.

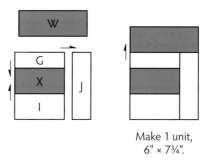

Make 1 unit, 6" × 7¾".

Build Your Stash

Start collecting red fabrics whenever you visit a quilt shop. Then when you make a quilt that calls for assorted red prints, you'll have a stash of similar red shades for a scrappy yet cohesive look. As I stitched this quilt, I enjoyed remembering where I discovered each of the red fabrics I was using. It's a trip down memory lane!

7 Join the units from steps 5 and 6. Sew the unit from step 4 to the left side to make the bottom unit, which should measure 14½" × 24½", including seam allowances.

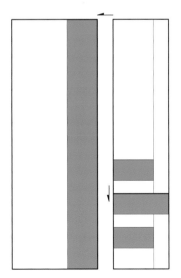

Make 1 bottom unit,
14½" × 24½".

8 Join the key top and bottom units to make the key section, which should measure 14½" × 34½", including seam allowances.

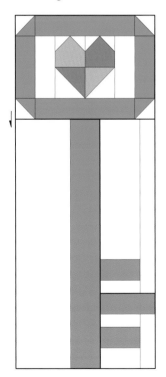

Make 1 key section,
14½" × 34½".

Making the *LOVE* Section

1   Lay out the white K, red I, red J, and white L pieces. Join all the pieces to make one *L* block measuring 6½" × 7½", including seam allowances.

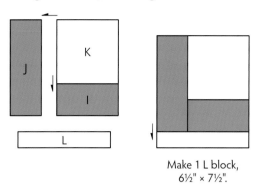

Make 1 L block,
6½" × 7½".

2   Draw a diagonal line from corner to corner on the wrong side of the white M squares. Layer a marked square on a pink M, right sides together. Sew ¼" from both sides of the drawn line. Cut the unit apart on the marked line. Make four half-square-triangle units and trim them to 2" square, including seam allowances.

Make 4 units.

3   Lay out the half-square-triangle units, the pink Z pieces, one white N square, and one white L strip. Join all the pieces to make an *O* block measuring 6½" × 7½", including seam allowances.

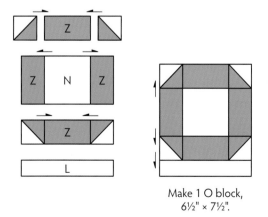

Make 1 O block,
6½" × 7½".

4   Draw a diagonal line from corner to corner on the wrong side of the remaining white N and the O squares. Layer a marked N square on one end of a red Y piece. Sew on the marked line. Trim the excess corner fabric ¼" from the stitched line. Place a marked O square on the other end of the red piece, noting the direction of the marked line. Sew and trim as before to make a unit measuring 3½" × 6½", including seam allowances. Repeat to make a mirror-image unit, noting the direction of the marked lines.

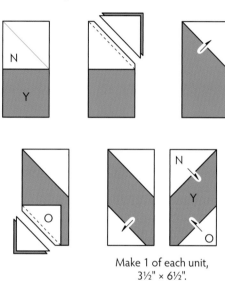

Make 1 of each unit,
3½" × 6½".

5   Join the units from step 4 and then sew a white L strip to the bottom edge to make a *V* block measuring 6½" × 7½", including seam allowances.

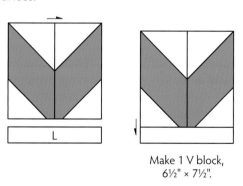

Make 1 V block,
6½" × 7½".

6   Lay out the pink G and D, white P, white Q, pink AA pieces, and one white L strip as shown. Join AA and Q and then add P and G. Sew D to the left

Key to My Heart

edge and L to the bottom to make an *E* block measuring 6½" × 7½", including seam allowances.

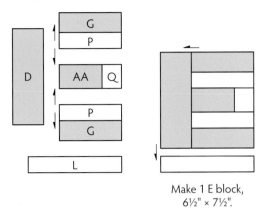

Make 1 E block,
6½" × 7½".

7 Join the *L, O, V,* and *E* blocks. Sew the remaining Heart block to the bottom edge to make a column measuring 6½" × 34½", including seam allowances.

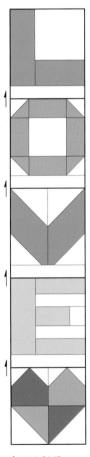

Make 1 LOVE section,
6½" × 34½".

Assembling the Quilt Top

1 Draw a diagonal line from corner to corner on the wrong side of two white C squares. Layer a marked square on a pink C, right sides together. Make four triangle units as described in step 2 on page 24 and trim them to 2½" square, including seam allowances.

Make 4 units.

2 Referring to the quilt assembly diagram below, join the white R strips alternately with the key section and *LOVE* column. The quilt top should measure 26½" × 34½", including seam allowances.

3 Sew triangle units to both ends of the white S strips to make the top and bottom borders,

which should measure 2½" × 26½". Sew the borders to the top and bottom edges. The quilt top should measure 26½" × 38½".

Finishing the Quilt

For more details on any finishing steps, visit ShopMartingale.com/HowtoQuilt for free downloadable information.

1 Layer the quilt top with batting and backing; baste the layers together.

2 Quilt by hand or machine. The quilt shown is machine quilted with a swirl design in the background. A heart design is stitched in the outer border and in the Heart blocks. Circles are stitched in the key and a variety of straight line designs are stitched in the letter blocks.

3 Use the red 2¼"-wide strips to make double-fold binding. Attach the binding to the quilt.

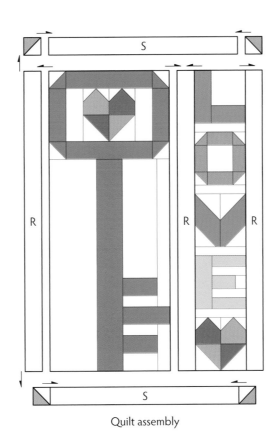

Quilt assembly

Lucky Charms

FINISHED QUILT: 20½" × 46½" • **FINISHED BLOCKS: 12" × 16" and 16" × 16"**

I never knew I had Irish roots until I traveled to Ireland. While there, the Irish people assumed my husband, Gregg, and I were researching family ties, so they tried to help us find "our people." When we returned home, we decided to do some research. It turns out our last name, Sloan, is from an Irishman a long time ago. I also have some Irish ties on my mom's side. As they say, we're all "a little bit Irish," especially in spring when the bright green clover begins to bloom.

Materials

Yardage is based on 42"-wide fabric. Fat eighths measure 9" × 21".

- ⅞ yard of mottled cream print for blocks, sashing, and inner border
- 1 fat eighth of dark green print for Shamrock blocks
- ½ yard of green dot for blocks, outer border, and binding
- 10 fat eighths of assorted green prints for blocks
- 1½ yards of fabric for backing
- 27" × 53" piece of batting

Cutting

All measurements include ¼" seam allowances.

From the mottled cream print, cut:
1 strip, 5½" × 42"; crosscut into 4 squares, 5½" × 5½"
1 strip, 5" × 42"; crosscut into 4 squares, 5" × 5"
1 strip, 3" × 42"; crosscut into 9 squares, 3" × 3"
3 strips, 2½" × 42"; crosscut into:
    4 strips, 2½" × 12½"
    16 squares, 2½" × 2½"
5 strips, 1½" × 42"; crosscut *2 of the strips* into 4 strips,
    1½" × 16½"

From the dark green print, cut:
2 squares, 6½" × 6½"

Continued on page 30

Continued from page 29

From the green dot, cut:

4 strips, 2¼" × 42"

4 strips, 1½" × 42"; crosscut *1 of the strips* into 2 strips, 1½" × 18½"

From *each of 2* of the assorted green prints, cut:

2 squares, 5" × 5" (4 total)

From the remainder of the assorted green prints and green dot, cut a *total* of:

9 squares, 3" × 3"

52 squares, 2½" × 2½"

Making the Shamrock Blocks

Press seam allowances in the directions indicated by the arrows.

1. Draw a diagonal line from corner to corner on the wrong side of the cream 5½" squares. Place marked squares on opposite corners of a dark green 6½" square. Sew on the marked lines. Trim the excess corner fabric ¼" from the stitched lines. Make two stem units measuring 6½" square, including seam allowances.

Make 2 stem units, 6½" × 6½".

2. Draw a diagonal line from corner to corner on the wrong side of the cream 3" squares. Layer a marked square on a green 3" square, right sides together. Sew ¼" from both sides of the drawn line. Cut the unit apart on the marked line. Make 18 half-square-triangle units and trim them to 2½" square, including seam allowances.

2½"

2½"

Make 18 units.

Fun Days to Celebrate in March

March 1: *National Umbrella Month begins*

First Friday in March: *National Day of Unplugging*

March 10: *National Pack Your Lunch Day*

March 16: *National Panda Day*

March 17: *St. Patrick's Day*

March 25: *International Waffle Day*

3 Lay out three half-square-triangle units and six green 2½" squares in three rows as shown. Sew the pieces into rows and then join the rows. Make six petal units measuring 6½" square, including seam allowances.

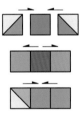

Make 6 petal units,
6½" × 6½".

4 Join three petal units and one stem unit. Make two units measuring 12½" square, including seam allowances.

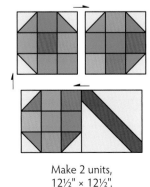

Make 2 units,
12½" × 12½".

5 Sew cream 2½" × 12½" strips to the top and bottom of the units from step 4 to make two Shamrock blocks measuring 12½" × 16½", including seam allowances.

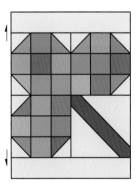

Make 2 Shamrock blocks,
12½" × 16½".

Celebrating Green!

If you love green, consider making five Shamrock blocks and four Double Four Patch Chain blocks to make a wall hanging that has Shamrocks in the center and four corners.

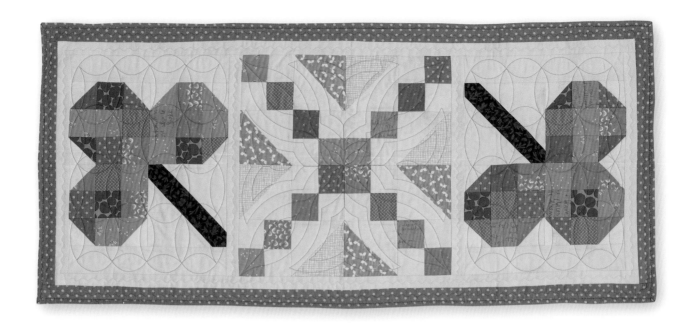

Making the Double Four Patch Chain Blocks

1 Draw a diagonal line from corner to corner on the wrong side of the cream 5" squares. Layer a marked square on a green 5" square, right sides together. Sew ¼" from both sides of the drawn line. Cut the unit apart on the marked line. Make two sets of four matching half-square-triangle units and trim them to 4½" square, including seam allowances.

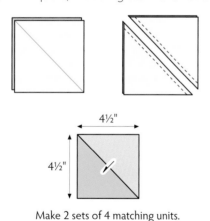

4½"
4½"

Make 2 sets of 4 matching units.

2 Lay out two green and two cream 2½" squares in two rows. Sew the squares into rows and then join the rows to make a four-patch unit. Make eight units measuring 4½" square, including seam allowances.

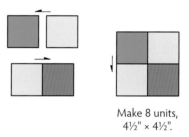

Make 8 units,
4½" × 4½".

3 Lay out two four-patch units and two matching half-square-triangle units in two rows as shown. Sew the units into rows and then join the rows. Make four units measuring 8½" square, including seam allowances.

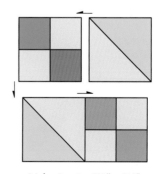

Make 4 units, 8½" × 8½".

4 Lay out the units from step 3 in two rows as shown, placing matching green triangles in diagonally opposite corners. Sew the units into rows and then join the rows to make a Double Four Patch Chain block measuring 16½" square, including seam allowances.

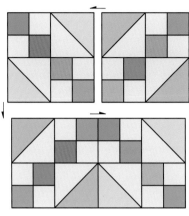

Make 1 Double Four Patch Chain block, 16½" × 16½".

Assembling the Table Runner

1 Referring to the table-runner assembly diagram below, lay out the blocks and the cream 1½" × 16½" strips, placing the Double Four Patch block in the center. Join the blocks and strips to make a row measuring 16½" × 44½", including seam allowances.

2 Join the remaining cream 1½"-wide strips end to end. From the pieced strip, cut two 44½"-long strips. Sew the strips to the long sides of the table runner. The runner should measure 18½" × 44½", including seam allowances.

3 Sew the green dot 1½" × 18½" strips to the short ends of the runner. Join the remaining green dot 1½"-wide strips end to end. From the pieced strip, cut two 46½"-long strips. Sew the strips to the long sides of the table runner. The runner should measure 20½" × 46½".

Finishing the Table Runner

For more details on any finishing steps, visit ShopMartingale.com/HowtoQuilt for free downloadable information.

1 Layer the runner top with batting and backing; baste the layers together.

2 Quilt by hand or machine. The table runner shown is machine quilted with a pumpkin-seed design in the Shamrock blocks and a flower motif in the Double Four Patch block. Wiggly lines are stitched in the sashing and borders.

3 Use the green dot 2¼"-wide strips to make double-fold binding. Attach the binding to the table runner.

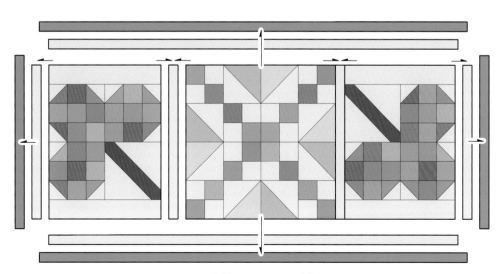

Table-runner assembly

Perk Up!

FINISHED QUILT: 8½" × 16" • **FINISHED BLOCKS: 4" × 4" and 8" × 10"**

If you've been with me for even a few days, you know I love coffee, and that's no fooling! It's the beverage I wake up with and the one I have for my afternoon break. I adore meeting friends for coffee and enjoy having coffee with my younger brother, Tom. We take a drive, pick up a coffee, and fix the problems of the world. Though International Coffee Day is October 1, I had to include a coffee quilt because I celebrate coffee **every day!**

Materials

Yardage is based on 42"-wide fabric. Fat eighths measure 9" × 21".

- 7" × 7" square of light print for Pinwheel blocks
- ¼ yard of pink dot for Pinwheel blocks, hearts, and binding
- 2" × 5" piece of yellow dot for coffee
- 6" × 8" piece of gray floral for cup and handle
- 3" × 7" piece of gray check for saucer
- 8½" × 10½" piece of blue print for appliqué background
- 2" × 8½" strip of pink print for setting
- 1 fat quarter of fabric for backing
- 12" × 19" piece of batting
- ¼ yard of 16"-wide paper-backed fusible web
- 50-weight thread in colors to match appliqués
- 5 yellow buttons, ¼" in diameter, for appliqué background
- 7 blue buttons, ⅛" to ⅜" in diameter, for coffee and setting strip
- 7 novelty buttons, ¼" to ¾" in diameter, for saucer, setting strip, and Pinwheel blocks

Cutting

All measurements include ¼" seam allowances.

From the light print, cut:

4 squares, 3" × 3"

From the pink dot, cut:

2 strips, 2¼" × 42"

4 squares, 3" × 3"

Making the Pinwheel Blocks

Press seam allowances in the directions indicated by the arrows.

1 Draw a diagonal line from corner to corner on the wrong side of the light squares. Layer a marked square on a pink dot square, right sides together. Sew ¼" from both sides of the drawn line. Cut the unit apart on the marked line. Make eight half-square-triangle units and trim them to 2½" square, including seam allowances.

2½" × 2½"

Make 8 units.

2 Lay out four half-square-triangle units in two rows, rotating the units to form a pinwheel. Sew the units into rows and then join the rows. Make two Pinwheel blocks measuring 4½" square, including seam allowances.

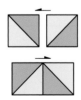

Make 2 Pinwheel blocks, 4½" × 4½".

Appliquéing the Coffee Cup Block

You can learn more about my fusible-appliqué techniques in my book *Pat Sloan's Teach Me to Appliqué* (Martingale, 2015).

1 Using the patterns on page 39, trace each shape the number of times indicated onto the fusible web. Roughly cut out each shape, about ½" beyond the drawn line. For larger shapes, such as the coffee cup, cut through the excess web around the shape, through the marked line, and into the interior of the shape. Cut away the excess fusible web on the *inside* of the shape, leaving about ¼" inside the drawn line.

2 Position the fusible-web shapes on the fabrics indicated on the patterns. Fuse as instructed by the manufacturer. Cut out the shapes on the marked line and remove the paper backing from each shape.

3 Referring to the appliqué placement diagram, position the prepared appliqué shapes on the blue piece, starting with the saucer.

8½"

10½"

Appliqué placement

4 Fuse the appliqués in place. Use matching thread to blanket-stitch around the outer edge of each shape.

Perk Up!

Fun Days to Celebrate in April

First Thursday in April: *National Burrito Day*

April 1: *April Fool's Day*

April 14: *National Gardening Day*

April 22: *Earth Day*

April 30: *National Adopt a Shelter Pet Day*

Assembling the Quilt Top

1 Join the two Pinwheel blocks to make a row measuring 4½" × 8½", including seam allowances.

2 Lay out the appliquéd block, the pink print 2" × 8½" strip, and the pinwheel row as shown in the quilt assembly diagram. Join the pieces to make the quilt top, which should measure 8½" × 16".

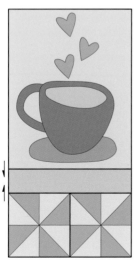

Quilt assembly

Finishing the Quilt

For more details on any finishing steps, visit ShopMartingale.com/HowtoQuilt for free downloadable information.

1 Layer the quilt top with batting and backing; baste the layers together.

2 Quilt by hand or machine. The quilt shown is machine quilted in the ditch around the appliqués and along the seamlines. Loops are stitched in the appliqué background and in the coffee cup.

3 Use the pink dot 2¼"-wide strips to make double-fold binding. Attach the binding to the quilt.

4 Sew a novelty button in the center of each pinwheel and in the right corner of the saucer. Sew four novelty buttons and one blue button on the pink strip. Sew yellow buttons around the hearts. Sew blue buttons in the center of the coffee as shown in the photo on page 37.

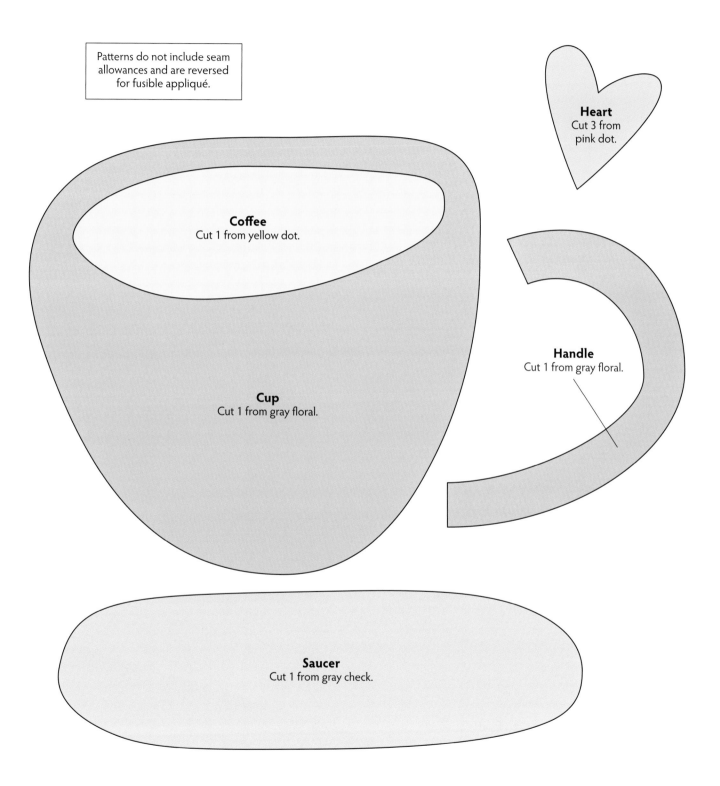

Patterns do not include seam allowances and are reversed for fusible appliqué.

Heart
Cut 3 from pink dot.

Coffee
Cut 1 from yellow dot.

Cup
Cut 1 from gray floral.

Handle
Cut 1 from gray floral.

Saucer
Cut 1 from gray check.

May Day

FINISHED QUILT: 46½" × 46½" • **FINISHED BLOCKS: 16" × 16"**

May 1 is May Day, an ancient celebration that signals the start of spring. It falls between the March equinox and June solstice. In earlier times there was singing and dancing, and celebrations included special bonfires. Animals and homes were decorated with May flowers and ribbons. These days we continue to welcome spring with flowers. One May my family visited Amsterdam and my dad got a great daffodil wreath for the front of the car. What fun!

Materials

Yardage is based on 42"-wide fabric. Fat eighths measure 9" × 21".

- ½ yard of white solid for blocks
- ¼ yard *each* of 2 green prints for blocks
- ½ yard *each* of light and dark gold prints for blocks
- 4 fat eighths of assorted light gray prints for blocks
- ¼ yard of gray dot for blocks
- ¾ yard of light floral for blocks and outer border
- ¼ yard *each* of 3 assorted blue prints for sashing
- ¾ yard of blue diagonal check for sashing, outer border, and binding
- 3 yards of fabric for backing
- 53" × 53" piece of batting

Cutting

All measurements include ¼" seam allowances.

From the white solid, cut:
3 strips, 3" × 42"; crosscut into 32 squares, 3" × 3"
1 strip, 2½" × 42"; crosscut into 16 squares, 2½" × 2½"

From *each* of the green prints, cut:
1 strip, 3" × 42"; crosscut into 8 squares, 3" × 3" (16 total)
1 strip, 2½" × 42"; crosscut into 8 squares, 2½" × 2½" (16 total)

Continued on page 42

Continued from page 41

From *each* of the gold prints, cut:

2 strips, 3" × 42"; crosscut into 16 squares, 3" × 3"
   (32 total)

2 strips, 2½" × 42"; crosscut into:
   8 pieces, 2½" × 4½" (16 total)
   16 squares, 2½" × 2½" (32 total)

1 strip, 2" × 42"; crosscut into 16 squares, 2" × 2"
   (32 total)

From *each* of the light gray prints, cut:

2 strips, 2½" × 21"; crosscut into:
   4 pieces, 2½" × 4½" (16 total)
   8 squares, 2½" × 2½" (32 total)

From the gray dot, cut:

2 strips, 2½" × 42"; crosscut into 16 pieces, 2½" × 4½"

From the light floral, cut:

5 strips, 4½" × 42"; crosscut into:
   4 strips, 4½" × 38½"
   4 squares, 4½" × 4½"

From *each* of the assorted blue prints, cut:

2 strips, 2½" × 42"; crosscut into 26 squares, 2½" × 2½"
   (78 total)

From the blue diagonal check, cut:

1 strip, 4½" × 42"; crosscut into 4 squares, 4½" × 4½"
2 strips, 2½" × 42"; crosscut into 27 squares, 2½" × 2½"
5 strips, 2¼" × 42"

Making the Half-Square-Triangle Units

Press seam allowances in the directions indicated by the arrows.

1   Draw a diagonal line from corner to corner on the wrong side of the white 3" squares. Layer a marked square on a green 3" square, right sides together. Sew ¼" from both sides of the drawn line. Cut the unit apart on the marked line. Make two sets

of 16 matching half-square-triangle units and trim them to 2½" square, including seam allowances.

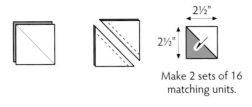

Make 2 sets of 16 matching units.

2 Repeat step 1 using the marked squares and the light and dark gold 3" squares to make 16 light gold units and 16 dark gold units.

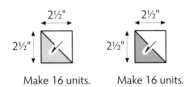

Make 16 units.   Make 16 units.

3 Draw a diagonal line from corner to corner on the wrong side of the remaining light gold 3" squares. Layer a marked square on a dark gold 3" square, right sides together. Sew ¼" from both sides of the drawn line. Cut the unit apart on the marked line. Make 16 half-square-triangle units and trim them to 2½" square, including seam allowances.

Make 16 units.

Making the Blocks

1 Lay out a white 2½" square, two matching green triangle units, one matching green 2½" square, a light gold triangle unit, a dark gold triangle unit, a light gold 2½" square, a dark gold 2½" square, and a light/dark gold triangle unit in three rows as shown above right. Sew all the pieces into rows and

then join the rows. Make two sets of four matching flower units measuring 6½" square, including seam allowances.

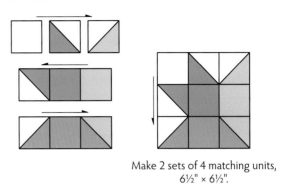

Make 2 sets of 4 matching units, 6½" × 6½".

2 Repeat step 1, reversing the position of the light and dark gold pieces to make a mirror-image flower unit. Make two sets of four matching mirror-image units measuring 6½" square, including seam allowances.

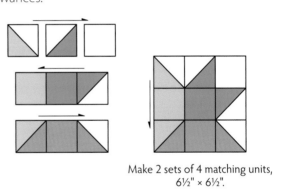

Make 2 sets of 4 matching units, 6½" × 6½".

3 Draw a diagonal line from corner to corner on the wrong side of the light gold 2" squares. Place a marked square on each end of a light gray piece, right sides together. Sew on the marked lines. Trim the excess corner fabric ¼" from the stitched lines. Make four sets of two matching A units measuring 2½" × 4½", including seam allowances.

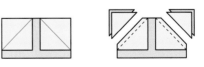

Make 4 sets of 2 matching A units, 2½" × 4½".

4 Draw a diagonal line from corner to corner on the wrong side of the dark gold 2" squares. Repeat step 3 to make four sets of two matching B units measuring 2½" × 4½", including seam allowances.

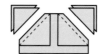

Make 4 sets of 2 matching B units, 2½" × 4½".

5 Draw a diagonal line from corner to corner on the wrong side of the light gray 2½" squares. Place a marked square on one end of a gray dot piece, right sides together. Sew on the marked line. Trim the excess corner fabric ¼" from the stitched line. Place a marked matching light gray square on the opposite end of the gray piece. Sew and trim as before to make a flying-geese unit measuring 2½" × 4½", including seam allowances. Make four sets of four matching units.

Make 4 sets of 4 matching units, 2½" × 4½".

6 Join a light gold piece, one A unit, and one matching flying-geese unit to make an A side unit. Make two A units. Join a dark gold piece, one B unit, and one matching flying-geese unit to make a B side unit. Make two B units. The light gray print should be the same in the A and B units. Repeat to make four sets of two matching A units and two

matching B units. The side units should measure 4½" × 6½", including seam allowances.

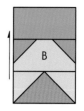

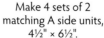

Make 4 sets of 2 matching A side units, 4½" × 6½".

Make 4 sets of 2 matching B side units, 4½" × 6½".

7 Lay out two flower units, two mirror-image flower units, two A side units, two B side units, and one light floral square in three rows as shown. The light gray print should match in all of the side units. Sew the pieces into rows and then join the rows. Make four blocks measuring 16½" square, including seam allowances.

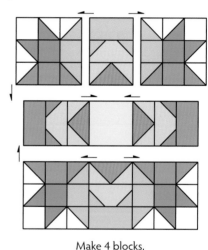

Make 4 blocks, 16½" × 16½".

Color Inspiration

When creating your quilt, choose the border print first. Then pick the flower color based on the border fabric, choosing two shades for the petals. I used golds, but maybe you prefer pink or red or purple. Rotating the blocks gives the design a playful look.

May Day

Assembling the Quilt Top

1 Referring to the photo on page 45, join eight blue print/check 2½" squares to make a strip. Make six strips measuring 2½" × 16½", including seam allowances.

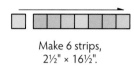

Make 6 strips,
2½" × 16½".

2 Join 19 blue print/check 2½" squares to make a strip. Make three strips measuring 2½" × 38½", including seam allowances.

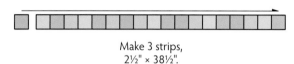

Make 3 strips,
2½" × 38½".

3 Referring to the quilt assembly diagram below, join two blocks and three strips from step 1. Make two block rows measuring 16½" × 38½", including seam allowances.

4 Join the block rows and strips from step 2, alternating their positions, to make the quilt top, which should measure 38½" square, including seam allowances.

5 Sew light floral 4½" × 38½" strips to the left and right sides of the quilt top. Sew blue check 4½" squares to both ends of one remaining light floral strip. Make two strips measuring 4½" × 46½", including seam allowances. Sew the strips to the top and bottom of the quilt top, which should measure 46½" square.

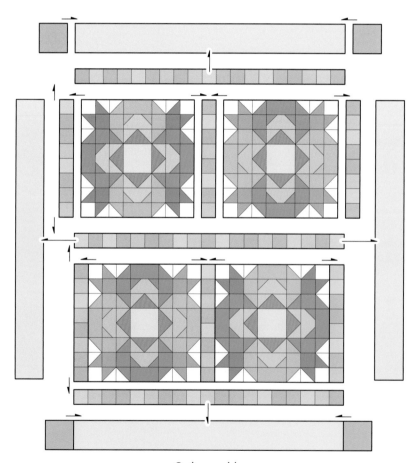

Quilt assembly

1st Sunday in May: *Mother's Day*

May 16: *National Do Something Good for Your Neighbor Day*

May 20: *National Pick Strawberries Day*

May 22: *National Solitaire Day*

May 24: *National Brother's Day*

Finishing the Quilt

For more details on any finishing steps, visit ShopMartingale.com/HowtoQuilt for free downloadable information.

1. Layer the quilt top with batting and backing; baste the layers together.

2. Quilt by hand or machine. The quilt shown is machine quilted with a floral design in the blocks. Circles are stitched in the sashing. A continuous floral design is stitched in the outer border.

3. Use the blue check 2¼"-wide strips to make double-fold binding. Attach the binding to the quilt.

Choosing Colors

Flowers are my greatest source of design inspiration. If you're stuck on color combinations, look at gardening websites, catalogs, and online groups. (Or go for a walk through your neighborhood!) One of my favorite sources for floral inspiration is the YouTube channel Garden Answer. Seeing all the amazing color combinations has me joyously digging into my fabrics every time!

Stars and Stripes

FINISHED QUILT: 68½" × 72½" • **FINISHED BLOCKS: 16" × 16" and 22" × 16"**

Materials

Yardage is based on 42"-wide fabric.

- 3⅜ yards of white print A for blocks, sashing, and border
- ⅝ yard of white print B for Sparkler blocks
- ¼ yard of white print C for Sparkler blocks
- 1⅜ yard of blue print for Sparkler blocks, sashing, and binding
- ½ yard of navy print for blocks
- ¼ yard of red dot for Sparkler blocks
- ⅓ yard *each* of 5 assorted red prints for Flag blocks
- ⅓ yard *each* of 4 assorted light prints for Flag blocks
- 4¼ yards of fabric for backing
- 75" × 79" piece of batting

Summertime is flag-waving season where I live. And this beauty can join the celebration from Flag Day (June 14) through the month of July. Create a quilt that's perfect for picnics and front porch sitting. As the song goes, "You're a grand old flag, you're a high-flying flag, and forever in peace may you wave."

Fun Days to Celebrate in June

First Friday in June: *National Doughnut Day*

June 3: *World Bicycle Day*

June 6: *National Yo-Yo Day*

June 10: *National Iced Tea Day*

June 13: *National Sewing Machine Day*

June 21: *National Seashell Day*

Cutting

All measurements include ¼" seam allowances.

From white print A, cut:

5 strips, 3" × 42"; crosscut into:
    8 strips, 3" × 16½"
    20 squares, 3" × 3"

32 strips, 2½" × 42"; crosscut *15 of the strips* into:
    2 strips, 2½" × 16½"
    8 strips, 2½" × 12"
    20 strips, 2½" × 6½"
    8 strips, 2½" × 6"
    20 pieces, 2½" × 4½"
    64 squares, 2½" × 2½"

8 strips, 1¾" × 42"; crosscut into
    8 strips, 1¾" × 22½"

From white print B, cut:

3 strips, 4½" × 42"; crosscut into
    20 squares, 4½" × 4½"

2 strips, 2½" × 42"; crosscut into
    20 squares, 2½" × 2½"

From white print C, cut:

1 strip, 4½" × 42"; crosscut into
    5 squares, 4½" × 4½"

From the blue print, cut:

2 strips, 3" × 42"; crosscut into
    20 squares, 3" × 3"

8 strips, 2½" × 42"; crosscut into:
    20 pieces, 2½" × 4½"
    76 squares, 2½" × 2½"

8 strips, 2¼" × 42"

From the navy print, cut:

1 strip, 10½" × 42"; crosscut into
    4 pieces, 8" × 10½"

2 strips, 2½" × 42"; crosscut into
    20 squares, 2½" × 2½"

From the red dot, cut:

3 strips, 2½" × 42"; crosscut into
    40 squares, 2½" × 2½"

From *each of 3* assorted red prints, cut:

2 strips, 2" × 42"; crosscut into
    4 strips, 2" × 12½" (12 total)

From *each of 2* of the assorted red prints, cut:

4 strips, 2" × 42"; crosscut into
    4 strips, 2" × 22½" (8 total)

From *each of 2* of the assorted light prints, cut:

2 strips, 2" × 42"; crosscut into
    4 strips, 2" × 12½" (8 total)

From *each of 2* of the assorted light prints, cut:

4 strips, 2" × 42"; crosscut into
    4 strips, 2" × 22½" (8 total)

     Pat Sloan's Holiday Hoopla

Making the Sparkler Blocks

Press seam allowances in the directions indicated by the arrows.

1 Draw a diagonal line from corner to corner on the wrong side of the white A 3" squares. Layer a marked square on a blue 3" square, right sides together. Sew ¼" from both sides of the drawn line. Cut the unit apart on the marked line. Make 40 half-square-triangle units and trim them to 2½" square, including seam allowances.

Make 40 units.

2 Lay out one navy square, two half-square-triangle units, and one white B 2½" square in two rows. Sew all the pieces into rows and then join the rows. Make 20 units measuring 4½" square, including seam allowances.

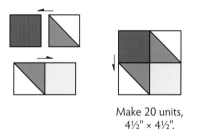

Make 20 units, 4½" × 4½".

3 Using the white A pieces, join a 2½" × 4½" and a 2½" × 6½" piece to a unit from step 2 as shown. Make 10 corner units and 10 mirror-image corner units measuring 6½" square, including seam allowances.

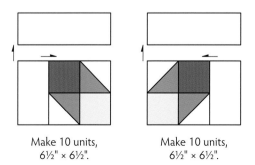

Make 10 units, 6½" × 6½".

Make 10 units, 6½" × 6½".

4 Draw a diagonal line from corner to corner on the wrong side of 40 white A 2½" squares. Place a marked square on one end of a blue piece, right sides together. Sew on the marked line. Trim the excess corner fabric ¼" from the stitched line. Place a marked square on the opposite end of the blue piece. Sew and trim as before. Make 20 flying-geese units measuring 2½" × 4½", including seam allowances.

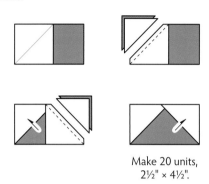

Make 20 units, 2½" × 4½".

5 Draw a diagonal line from corner to corner on the wrong side of 40 blue and all the red dot 2½" squares. Place marked blue and red squares on diagonally opposite corners of a white B 4½" square. Sew on the marked lines. Trim the excess corner fabric ¼" from the stitched lines. Place marked blue and red squares on the remaining corners of the white square. Sew and trim as before. Make 20 square-in-a-square units measuring 4½" square, including seam allowances.

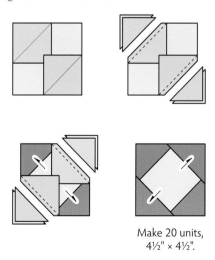

Make 20 units, 4½" × 4½".

6 Sew a flying-geese unit to the top of a square-in-a-square unit, placing the blue triangles next to each other. Make 20 side units measuring 4½" × 6½", including seam allowances.

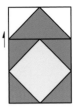

Make 20 side units,
4½" × 6½".

7 Lay out two corner units, two mirror-image corner units, four side units, and one white C square in three rows, rotating the units as shown. Sew the pieces into rows and then join the rows. Make five Sparkler blocks measuring 16½" square, including seam allowances.

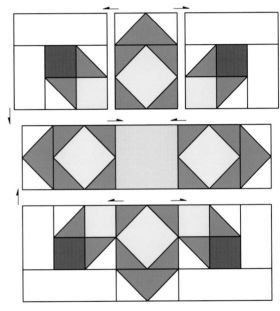

Make 5 Sparkler blocks,
16½" × 16½".

Making the Flag Blocks

1 Join three different red and two different light 2" × 12½" strips, alternating them as shown. Make four strip units measuring 8" × 12½", including seam allowances.

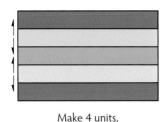

Make 4 units,
8" × 12½".

2 Join two different light and two different red 2" × 22½" strips, alternating them as shown. Make four strip units measuring 6½" × 22½", including seam allowances.

Make 4 units,
6½" × 22½".

3 Join a navy piece to a unit from step 1. Sew this unit to the top of the step 2 unit. Sew white A 1¾" × 22½" strips to the top and bottom edges. Make four Flag blocks measuring 22½" × 16½", including seam allowances.

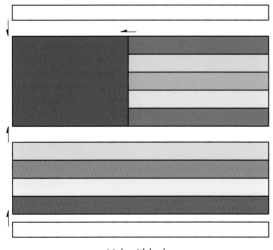

Make 4 blocks,
22½" × 16½".

Making the Sashing Rows

1 Join three blue and two white A 2½" squares. Make 12 units measuring 2½" × 10½", including seam allowances.

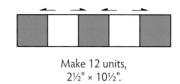

Make 12 units,
2½" × 10½".

2 Join two white A 2½" × 6" strips, three units from step 1, and two white A 2½" × 12" strips. Make four strips measuring 2½" × 64½", including seam allowances.

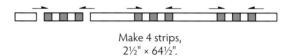

Make 4 strips,
2½" × 64½".

3 Join 13 white A 2½" × 42" strips end to end. Cut eight 64½"-long strips from the long pieced strip.

4 Join one strip from step 2 and two strips from step 3 to make a sashing row. Make four sashing rows measuring 6½" × 64½", including seam allowances.

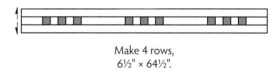

Make 4 rows,
6½" × 64½".

Mix It Up

Mixing scrappy and non-scrappy (or planned) blocks makes this quilt sparkle. I used a variety of fabrics for the Flag blocks, but for the Sparkler blocks, I used the same five fabrics consistently in each block. This gives the quilt a balanced look with the chance to still use a lot of fun fabrics.

Assembling the Quilt Top

Refer to the quilt assembly diagram below as needed throughout.

1 Join four white A 3" × 16½" strips, two Sparkler blocks, and one Flag block to make a block row measuring 16½" × 64½", including seam allowances. Repeat to make a second row.

2 Join two Flag blocks, two white A 2½" × 16½" strips, and one Sparkler block to make a block row measuring 16½" × 64½", including seam allowances.

3 Join the sashing rows and block rows, alternating them as shown. The quilt top should measure 64½" × 72½", including seam allowances.

4 Join the remaining white A 2½" × 42" strips end to end. From the pieced strip, cut two 72½"-long strips. Sew the strips to the left and right sides of the quilt top. The quilt top should measure 68½" × 72½".

Finishing the Quilt

For more details on any finishing steps, visit ShopMartingale.com/HowtoQuilt for free downloadable information.

1 Layer the quilt top with batting and backing; baste the layers together.

2 Quilt by hand or machine. The quilt shown is machine quilted with horizontal wavy lines from edge to edge.

3 Use the blue 2¼"-wide strips to make double-fold binding. Attach the binding to the quilt.

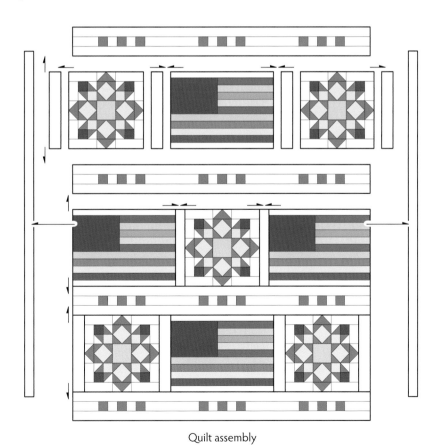

Quilt assembly

Ice Cream Social

FINISHED TABLE RUNNER: 20½" × 44½" • **FINISHED BLOCK: 12" × 12"**

As a child, I thought the best sound of summer was the jingle of the ice cream truck. I'd order an orange Creamsicle, and my brother would choose sky-blue popsicles. His mouth was blue for hours! As an homage to those memories, I combined orange and blue for a Log Cabin runner celebrating Ice Cream Day on the third Sunday in July—or any time of year. Pull out your favorite summer "ice cream colors" to make yours!

Materials

Yardage is based on 42"-wide fabric. Fat eighths measure 9" × 21".

- ⅓ yard of white solid for blocks
- 4 fat eighths of assorted orange prints for blocks
- 4 fat eighths of assorted blue prints for blocks
- ⅞ yard of dark blue dot for blocks, outer border, and binding
- ¼ yard of orange stripe for inner border
- 1½ yards of fabric for backing
- 27" × 51" piece of batting

Cutting

All measurements include ¼" seam allowances.

From the white solid, cut:
4 strips, 2" × 42"; crosscut into:
    12 pieces, 2" × 5"
    12 pieces, 2" × 3½"
    12 squares, 2" × 2"

From the assorted orange prints, cut a *total* of:
6 pieces, 2" × 6½"
6 pieces, 2" × 5"
6 pieces, 2" × 3½"
6 squares, 2" × 2"

Continued on page 58

Continued from page 57

From the assorted blue prints, cut a *total* of:

6 pieces, 2" × 6½"

6 pieces, 2" × 5"

6 pieces, 2" × 3½"

6 squares, 2" × 2"

From the dark blue dot, cut:

4 strips, 3½" × 42"; crosscut into:

    2 strips, 3½" × 38½"

    2 strips, 3½" × 20½"

4 strips, 2¼" × 42"

1 strip, 2" × 42"; crosscut into 12 squares, 2" × 2"

From the orange stripe, cut:

3 strips, 1½" × 42"; crosscut into:

    2 strips, 1½" × 36½"

    2 strips, 1½" × 14½"

Making the Blocks

Press seam allowances in the directions indicated by the arrows.

1 Join one orange square and one white square to make a two-patch unit. Sew a blue 2" × 3½" piece to the bottom of a two-patch unit. Make six units measuring 3½" square, including seam allowances.

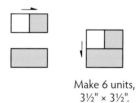

Make 6 units, 3½" × 3½".

2 Sew a white 2" × 3½" piece to the left edge of a unit from step 1. Sew a white 2" × 5" piece to the top edge. Make six units measuring 5" square, including seam allowances.

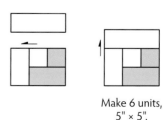

Make 6 units, 5" × 5".

3 Sew a blue 2" × 5" piece to the right edge and an orange 2" × 6½" piece to the bottom edge. Make six A units measuring 6½" square, including seam allowances.

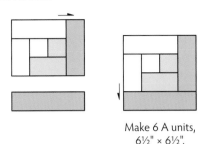

Make 6 A units,
6½" × 6½".

4 Repeat steps 1–3 using the blue squares, orange 2" × 3½" and 2" × 5" pieces, the blue 2" × 6½" pieces, and the remaining white squares and pieces to make six B units measuring 6½" square, including seam allowances.

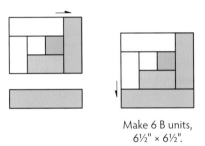

Make 6 B units,
6½" × 6½".

5 Draw a diagonal line from corner to corner on the wrong side of the dark blue squares. Place a marked square on the darker corner of an A unit, right sides together. Sew on the marked line. Trim the excess corner fabric ¼" from the stitched line. Make two A units measuring 6½" square, including seam allowances.

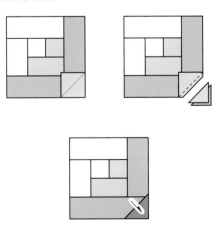

Make 2 A units,
6½" × 6½".

Fun Days to Celebrate in July

First Saturday in July: *Hop-a-Park Day*

July 11: *National Blueberry Muffin Day and National Mojito Day*

    (or just put blueberries in your mojito!)

July 14: *National Tape Measure Day*

July 20: *World Jump Day*

July 24: *National Tell an Old Joke Day*

July 30: *International Friendship Day*

6 Place a marked dark blue square on the darker corner of a B unit, right sides together. Sew on the marked line. Trim the excess corner fabric ¼" from the stitched line. Make six B units measuring 6½" square, including seam allowances.

7 Place a marked dark blue square on the white corner of an A unit, right sides together. Sew on the marked line. Trim the excess corner fabric ¼" from the stitched line. Make four C units measuring 6½" square, including seam allowances.

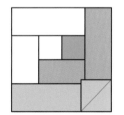 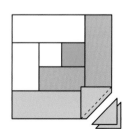

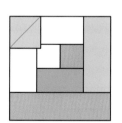 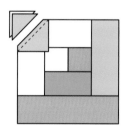

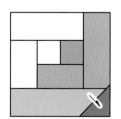

Make 6 B units,
6½" × 6½".

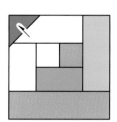

Make 4 C units,
6½" × 6½".

8 Lay out one A unit and three B units, rotating them as shown. Sew the units into rows; join the rows. Make two blocks measuring 12½" square, including seam allowances.

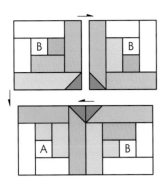

Make 2 blocks, 12½" × 12½".

9 Lay out the C units, rotating them so the dark blue triangles are in the center. Sew the units into rows and then join the rows to make a block measuring 12½" square, including seam allowances.

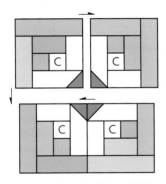

Make 1 block, 12½" × 12½".

Assembling the Table Runner

1 Referring to the table-runner assembly diagram below, join the three blocks. The runner should measure 12½" × 36½", including seam allowances.

2 Sew the orange stripe 1½" × 36½" strips to the long sides of the runner. Sew the orange stripe 1½" × 14½" strips to the short ends.

3 Sew the dark blue 3½" × 38½" strips to the long sides of the runner. Sew the dark blue 3½" × 20½" strips to the short ends. The table runner should measure 20½" × 44½".

Finishing the Table Runner

For more details on any finishing steps, visit ShopMartingale.com/HowtoQuilt for free downloadable information.

1 Layer the table-runner top with batting and backing; baste the layers together.

2 Quilt by hand or machine. The table runner shown is machine quilted with a flower motif in the dark area and pebbles in the light areas of the blocks. A wiggly line is stitched in the inner border and a meandering line is stitched in the outer border.

3 Use the dark blue 2¼"-wide strips to make double-fold binding. Attach the binding to the table runner.

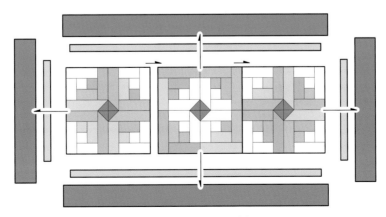

Table-runner assembly

Celebrate Friendship

FINISHED QUILT: 42½" × 42½" · **FINISHED BLOCK: 16" × 16"**

One of the wonderful things about being a quilter is meeting other quilters from around the world. The Internet has eliminated our communication gap. You can wake up in the morning, click on your phone, and see what your friend halfway across the world just created. And you don't need to speak the same language; we all speak quilts. I invite you to join my community, where quilters from every corner of the world meet daily.

Materials

Yardage is based on 42"-wide fabric. Fat eighths measure 9" × 21".

- 1 yard of pink solid for blocks and borders
- ⅓ yard of green print for blocks
- 1⅛ yards of black floral for blocks, borders, and binding
- 15 fat eighths of assorted light, medium, and dark prints (collectively referred to as "dark") for houses units
- 1 fat eighth of pink dot for border units
- 1 fat eighth of red diagonal stripe for border units
- ¼ yard of black dot for border
- 2¾ yards of fabric for backing
- 49" × 49" piece of batting

Cutting

All measurements include ¼" seam allowances.

From the pink solid, cut:
1 strip, 3" × 42"; crosscut into 12 squares, 3" × 3"
8 strips, 2½" × 42"; crosscut into:
    2 strips, 2½" × 20½"
    2 strips, 2½" × 16½"
    16 pieces, 2½" × 4½"
    60 squares, 2½" × 2½"
4 strips, 1½" × 42"; crosscut into:
    2 strips, 1½" × 34½"
    2 strips, 1½" × 32½"

Continued on page 64

Making the Center Block

Press seam allowances in the directions indicated by the arrows.

1 Draw a diagonal line from corner to corner on the wrong side of eight pink solid 3" squares. Layer a marked square on a green 3" square, right sides together. Sew ¼" from both sides of the drawn line. Cut the unit apart on the marked line. Make 16 half-square-triangle units and trim them to 2½" square, including seam allowances.

Make 16 units.

2 Lay out one pink solid 2½" × 4½" piece, two pink solid 2½" squares, one green 2½" square, and four half-square-triangle units as shown. Sew all the pieces into columns and then join the columns. Make four corner units measuring 6½" square, including seam allowances.

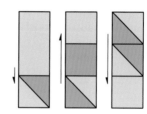 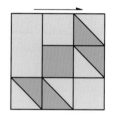

Make 4 corner units, 6½" × 6½".

3 Draw a diagonal line from corner to corner on the wrong side of eight green, eight pink solid, and the black floral 2½" squares. Place a marked green square on one end of a pink solid 2½" × 4½" piece, right sides together. Sew on the marked line. Trim the excess corner fabric ¼" from the stitched line. Place a marked green square on the opposite end of the pink piece. Sew and trim as before to make a flying-geese unit. Make four green/pink units measuring 2½" × 4½", including seam allowances. Use the marked pink solid squares and the green 2½" × 4½" pieces to make four

Continued from page 63

From the green print, cut:
1 strip, 3" × 42"; crosscut into 8 squares, 3" × 3"
2 strips, 2½" × 42"; crosscut into:
    4 pieces, 2½" × 4½"
    12 squares, 2½" × 2½"

From the black floral, cut:
5 strips, 3½" × 42"; crosscut *2 of the strips* into 2 strips, 3½" × 36½"
1 strip, 2½" × 42"; crosscut into 8 squares, 2½" × 2½"
5 strips, 2¼" × 42"
1 square, 4½" × 4½"

From *each of 12* assorted dark prints, cut:
2 pieces, 1¾" × 4½" (24 total)
1 piece, 1¾" × 2" (12 total)

From the remainder of the assorted dark prints, cut a *total* of:
8 squares, 4½" × 4½"
20 pieces, 2½" × 4½"
12 pieces, 2" × 3¼"

From the pink dot, cut:
4 squares, 3" × 3"
4 squares, 2½" × 2½"

From the red diagonal stripe, cut:
8 squares, 3" × 3"
4 squares, 2½" × 2½"

From the black dot, cut:
2 strips, 1½" × 36½"
2 strips, 1½" × 34½"

pink/green units. Use the marked black floral squares and pink solid 2½" × 4½" pieces to make four black/pink units.

Make 4 units,
2½" × 4½".

Make 4 units,
2½" × 4½".

Make 4 units,
2½" × 4½".

4 Join one of each unit from step 3 to make a side unit. Make four units measuring 4½" × 6½", including seam allowances.

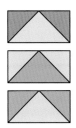 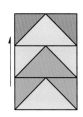

Make 4 side units,
4½" × 6½".

5 Lay out the corner units, side units, and the black floral 4½" square in three rows. Sew the pieces into rows and then join the rows to make a block measuring 16½" square, including seam allowances.

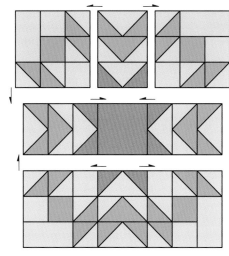

Make 1 block, 16½" × 16½".

Making the House Border

1 To make a roof, draw a diagonal line from corner to corner on the wrong side of 40 pink solid 2½" squares. Place a marked square on one end of a dark 2½" × 4½" piece, right sides together. Sew on the marked line. Trim the excess corner fabric ¼" from the stitched line. Place a marked square on the opposite end of the piece. Sew and trim as before to make a flying-geese unit. Make 20 units measuring 2½" × 4½", including seam allowances.

Make 20 units,
2½" × 4½".

2 To make a house front, join one dark 1¾" × 2" and one dark 2" × 3¼" piece from a different print to make a center strip. Sew matching dark 1¾" × 4½" pieces to opposite sides of the strip. Make 12 units measuring 4½" square, including seam allowances.

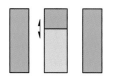

Make 12 units,
4½" × 4½".

3 Sew a roof to the top of a house front to make a house A unit. Make 12 units measuring 4½" × 6½", including seam allowances.

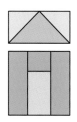 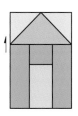

Make 12 house A units,
4½" × 6½".

4 Join a roof and a dark 4½" square to make a house B unit. Make eight units measuring 4½" × 6½", including seam allowances.

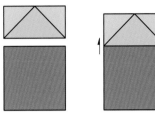

Make 8 house B units,
4½" × 6½".

5 Draw a diagonal line from corner to corner on the wrong side of the remaining pink solid and the pink dot 3" squares. Layer a marked square on a red stripe 3" square, right sides together. Sew ¼" from both sides of the drawn line. Cut the unit apart on the marked line. Make 16 half-square-triangle units and trim them to 2½" square, including seam allowances.

Make 16 units.

6 Lay out one pink solid 2½" × 4½" piece, a pink solid and a red stripe 2½" square, two red/pink half-square-triangle units, two red/pink dot half-square-triangle units, and one pink dot 2½" square as shown. Sew all the pieces into columns and then join the columns. Make four corner units measuring 6½" square, including seam allowances.

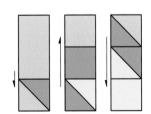 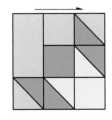

Make 4 corner units,
6½" × 6½".

7 Join three house A and two house B units to make a side border that measures 6½" × 20½", including seam allowances. Make two. Make two more borders in the same way, adding a corner unit to each end. The top and bottom borders should measure 6½" × 32½", including seam allowances.

Make 2 side borders, 6½" × 20½".

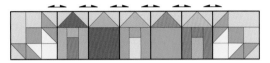

Make 2 top/bottom borders, 6½" × 32½".

Assembling the Quilt Top

Refer to the quilt assembly diagram on page 67 as needed throughout.

1 Sew pink solid 2½" × 16½" strips to the top and bottom edges of the center block. Sew pink solid 2½" × 20½" strips to the left and right sides. The quilt top should measure 20½" square, including seam allowances.

2 Sew the shorter house borders to the left and right sides of the quilt top. Sew the longer house borders to the top and bottom edges. The quilt top should measure 32½" square, including seam allowances.

3 Sew pink solid 1½" × 32½" strips to the top and bottom edges of the quilt top. Sew pink solid 1½" × 34½" strips to the left and right sides. The quilt top should measure 34½" square, including seam allowances.

4 Sew black dot 1½" × 34½" strips to the top and bottom edges of the quilt top. Sew black dot 1½" × 36½" strips to the left and right sides. The quilt top should measure 36½" square, including seam allowances.

Fun Days to Celebrate in August

First Sunday in August: *National Friendship Day*

August 1: *National Spider-Man Day*

August 6: *National Root Beer Float Day*

August 12: *World Elephant Day*

August 17: *National Thrift Shop Day*

5 Sew black floral 3½" × 36½" strips to the top and bottom edges of the quilt top. Join the remaining black floral 3½"-wide strips end to end. From the pieced strips, cut two 42½"-long strips and sew them to the left and right sides. The quilt top should measure 42½" square.

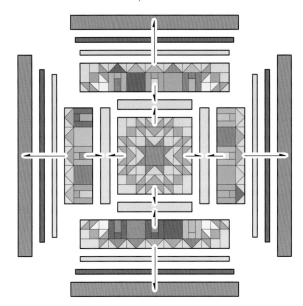

Quilt assembly

Finishing the Quilt

For more details on any finishing steps, visit ShopMartingale.com/HowtoQuilt for free downloadable information.

1 Layer the quilt top with batting and backing; baste the layers together.

2 Quilt by hand or machine. The quilt shown is machine quilted with an allover Baptist fan design.

3 Use the black floral 2¼"-wide strips to make double-fold binding. Attach the binding to the quilt.

Love Your Library

Books, books, glorious books! Celebrate reading every day, but especially on Read-a-Book Day, September 6. When I was a kid, I read all kinds of books, from Pearl S. Buck's depiction of life in China to as many Agatha Christie mysteries as I could get a hold of. The library was my go-to spot after school. Leaving with a big stack of books to read was the best feeling ever. Make the books in this quilt your own by finding fabrics that remind you of your favorite books.

Materials

Yardage is based on 42"-wide fabric.

- ⅝ yard of mottled white print for blocks and setting
- 1 yard *total* of assorted prints for blocks
- 1 yard of navy stripe for sashing and inner border
- 6" × 6" square of blue print for cornerstones
- 1 yard of teal floral for outer border and binding
- 2¾ yards of fabric for backing
- 49" × 57" piece of batting

Cutting

All measurements include ¼" seam allowances. As you cut, label the pieces as indicated for easy assembly.

From the mottled white print, cut:
1 strip, 12½" × 42"; crosscut into:
    1 strip, 5½" × 12½" (E)
    2 strips, 3½" × 12½" (F)
    1 strip, 2½" × 12½" (G)
    3 strips, 2½" × 11½" (D)
2 strips, 2½" × 42"; crosscut into:
    10 pieces, 2½" × 3½" (B)
    6 squares, 2½" × 2½" (C)
2 strips, 1½" × 42"; crosscut into 21 pieces,
    1½" × 2½" (A)

Continued on page 70

Fun Days to Celebrate in September

September 1: *World Letter Writing Day*

September 8: *International Literacy Day*

September 9: *International Sudoku Day*

September 24: *National Bluebird of Happiness Day*

September 29: *World Heart Day*

Continued from page 69

From the assorted prints, cut a *total* of:

10 strips, 2½" × 11½" (D)

3 strips, 2½" × 10½" (H)

10 strips, 2½" × 9½" (I)

8 strips, 2½" × 9" (J)

5 strips, 2½" × 7½" (K)

1 strip, 2½" × 7" (L)

3 strips, 2½" × 6" (M)

1 square, 2½" × 2½" (C)

22 pieces, 2" × 2½" (N)

11 pieces, 1½" × 2½" (A)

From the navy stripe, cut on the *lengthwise* grain:

4 strips, 2½" × 32½"

4 strips, 2½" × 14½"

2 strips, 2½" × 12½"

From the blue print, cut:

4 squares, 2½" × 2½"

From the teal floral, cut:

5 strips, 3½" × 42"; trim *2 of the strips* to 36½" long

5 strips, 2¼" × 42"

Making the Blocks

Press seam allowances in the directions indicated by the arrows.

1 For block A, lay out the pieces listed below in four columns. Sew all the pieces into columns and then join the columns. Make five blocks measuring 8½" × 12½", including seam allowances.

- **White:** two A, one B, and one C

- **Assorted prints:** one A, one D, one I, one J, one K, and three N

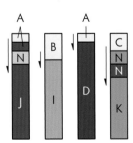
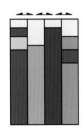

Make 5 A blocks,
8½" × 12½".

2 For block B, lay out the pieces listed below in six rows. Sew all the pieces into rows and then join the rows. Make three blocks measuring 11½" × 12½", including seam allowances.

- **White:** three A, one B, and one D
- **Assorted prints:** two A, one D, one H, one I, one J, one M, and two N

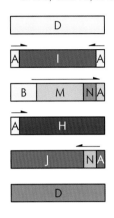
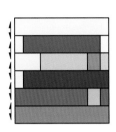

Make 3 B blocks, 11½" × 12½".

3 For block C, lay out the pieces listed below in five columns. Sew all the pieces into columns and then join the columns. Make one block measuring 10½" × 12½", including seam allowances.

- **White:** two A, two B, and one C
- **Assorted prints:** one C, two D, two I, one L, and one N

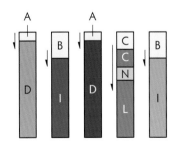
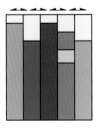

Make 1 C block, 10½" × 12½".

Assembling the Quilt Top

1 Join two A blocks, one B block, and one white E piece to make the top row, which should measure 12½" × 32½", including seam allowances.

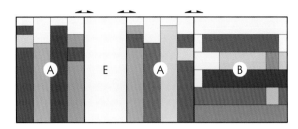

Make 1 top row, 12½" × 32½".

2 Join one A block, one B block, one C block, and one white F piece to make the center row, which should measure 12½" × 32½", including seam allowances.

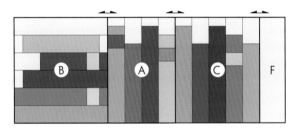

Make 1 middle row, 12½" × 32½".

3 Join two A blocks, one B block, one white F piece, and one white G piece to make the bottom row, which should measure 12½" × 32½", including seam allowances.

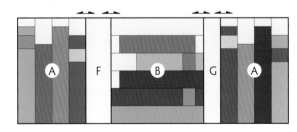

Make 1 bottom row, 12½" × 32½".

4 Referring to the quilt assembly diagram on page 73, join the block rows and navy 2½" × 32½" strips, alternating their positions as shown. The quilt top should measure 32½" × 44½", including seam allowances.

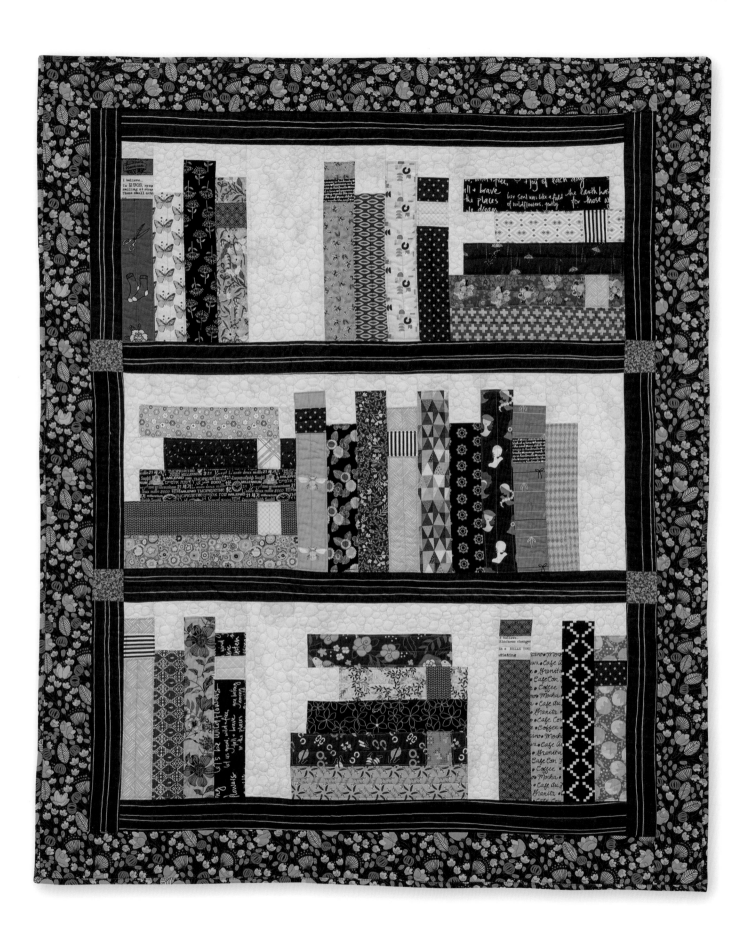

Pat Sloan's Holiday Hoopla

5 Join two navy 2½" × 14½" strips, one navy 2½" × 12½" strip, and two blue squares to make a side border measuring 2½" × 44½", including seam allowances. Make two borders and sew them to the left and right sides of the quilt top. The quilt top should measure 36½" × 44½", including seam allowances.

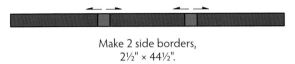

Make 2 side borders,
2½" × 44½".

6 Sew the teal 3½" × 36½" strips to the top and bottom edges of the quilt top. Join the remaining teal 3½"-wide strips end to end. From the pieced strip, cut two 50½"-long strips and sew them to the left and right sides. The quilt top should measure 42½" × 50½".

Finishing the Quilt

For more details on any finishing steps, visit ShopMartingale.com/HowtoQuilt for free downloadable information.

1 Layer the quilt top with batting and backing; baste the layers together.

2 Quilt by hand or machine. The quilt shown is machine quilted with pebbles in the background. Straight lines are stitched in the books and sashing. Meandering loops are stitched in the outer border.

3 Use the teal floral 2¼"-wide strips to make double-fold binding. Attach the binding to the quilt.

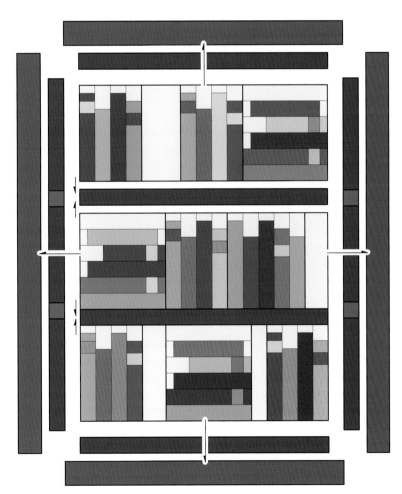

Quilt assembly

Pick a Pumpkin

FINISHED QUILT: 39½" × 39½" • **FINISHED BLOCK: 21" × 21"**

I love pumpkins—big ones, small ones, orange, white, and green ones. No matter what they look like, I adore pumpkins! Be sure to add pumpkin shopping to the top of the list for October, whether you're buying one for the front porch or buying the materials to make a fabric one. Pumpkin Day is October 26, and this quilt will pair perfectly with pumpkin spice lattes, pumpkin bread, and pumpkin pie!

Materials

Yardage is based on 42"-wide fabric. Fat eighths measure 9" × 21".

- 7" × 7" square of cream dot for Pumpkin block
- 3 fat eighths of assorted orange A prints for Pumpkin block
- 1⅛ yards of cream floral for blocks and border units
- 4½" × 4½" square of black print for Pumpkin block
- 6" × 11" piece of green A print for Pumpkin block and border units
- ½ yard of orange check for churn dash units and binding
- 3 pieces, 6" × 13" *each*, of assorted orange B prints for churn dash units
- ⅝ yard of green B print for border units, inner border, and outer border
- 2⅝ yards of fabric for backing
- 46" × 46" piece of batting

Cutting

All measurements include ¼" seam allowances. Keep like pieces together.

From the cream dot, cut:
3 squares, 3" × 3"
1 square, 2½" × 2½"

Continued on page 76

Fun Days to Celebrate in October

October 1: *Model T Day*

October 2: *National Fried Scallops Day*

October 18: *National Chocolate Cupcake Day*

October 20: *International Sloth Day*

Fourth Saturday in October: *National Make a Difference Day*

Continued from page 75

From *each* of the assorted orange A prints, cut:
1 square, 3" × 3" (3 total)
17 squares, 2½" × 2½" (51 total)

From the cream floral, cut:
1 strip, 4½" × 42"; crosscut into:
    1 piece, 4½" × 7¼"
    1 piece, 4½" × 5¾"
    3 squares, 4½" × 4½"
3 strips, 4" × 42"; crosscut into 16 pieces, 4" × 6½"
3 strips, 3" × 42"; crosscut into:
    2 strips, 3" × 21½"
    16 squares, 3" × 3"
2 strips, 2½" × 42"; crosscut into 27 squares, 2½" × 2½"
1 strip, 2" × 42"; crosscut into 2 strips, 2" × 16½"
2 strips, 1½" × 42"; crosscut into 32 pieces, 1½" × 2½"

From the green A print, cut:
8 squares, 2½" × 2½"

From the orange check, cut:
5 strips, 2¼" × 42"
4 squares, 3" × 3"
8 pieces, 1½" × 2½"

From *each* of the assorted orange B prints, cut:
4 squares, 3" × 3" (12 total)
8 pieces, 1½" × 2½" (24 total)

From the green B print, cut:
8 strips, 2" × 42"; crosscut into:
    2 strips, 2" × 39½"
    2 strips, 2" × 36½"
    2 strips, 2" × 24½"
    2 strips, 2" × 21½"
4 squares, 2½" × 2½"

Making the Pumpkin Block

Press seam allowances in the directions indicated by the arrows.

1 Draw a diagonal line from corner to corner on the wrong side of the cream dot 3" squares. Layer a marked square on an orange A 3" square, right sides together. Sew ¼" from both sides of the drawn line. Cut the unit apart on the marked line. Make six half-square-triangle units and trim them to 2½" square, including seam allowances. Two units will be extra.

Make 6 units.

2 Lay out the orange A 2½" squares, the cream dot 2½" square, and four half-square-triangle units in seven rows as shown. Sew the pieces into rows and then join the rows to make a checkerboard unit measuring 14½" × 16½", including seam allowances.

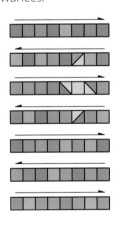 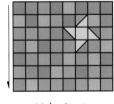

Make 1 unit,
14½" × 16½".

3 Draw a diagonal line from corner to corner on the wrong side of the cream floral 4½" and three cream floral 2½" squares. Place marked 4½" squares on the upper-left and upper-right corners of the checkerboard unit, right sides together. Place marked 2½" squares on the lower-left and lower-right corners of the unit. Sew on the marked lines. Trim the excess corner fabric ¼" from the stitched lines to make a unit measuring 14½" × 16½", including seam allowances.

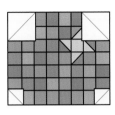 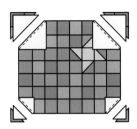

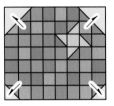

Make 1 unit,
14½" × 16½".

4 Layer the remaining marked cream floral 4½" square on top of the black square, right sides together. Sew on the marked lines. Trim the excess corner fabric ¼" from the stitched lines. Place a marked cream floral 2½" square on the corner of the black triangle. Sew and trim as before to make a stem unit measuring 4½" square, including seam allowances.

Make 1 unit,
4½" × 4½".

5 Join the cream floral 4½" × 5¾" piece, the stem unit, and the cream floral 4½" × 7¼" piece to make a row. Sew the row to the top of the unit from step 3 to make a pumpkin unit measuring 16½" × 18½", including seam allowances.

6 Sew cream floral 2" × 16½" strips to the top and bottom of the pumpkin unit. Sew cream floral 3" × 21½" strips to the left and right sides of the unit. The unit should measure 21½" square, including seam allowances.

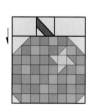

Make 1 unit,
16½" × 18½".

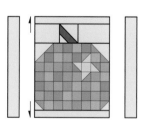
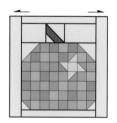

Make 1 unit,
21½" × 21½".

Pat Sloan's Holiday Hoopla

7 Draw a diagonal line from corner to corner on the wrong side of four green A squares. Place marked squares on the corners of the step 6 unit, right sides together. Sew on the marked lines. Trim the excess corner fabric ¼" from the stitched lines to complete the Pumpkin block. The block should measure 21½" square, including seam allowances.

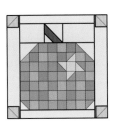 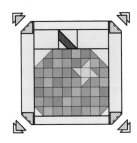

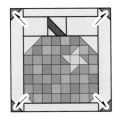

Make 1 Pumpkin block, 21½" × 21½".

Making the Churn Dash Border

1 Draw a diagonal line from corner to corner on the wrong side of the cream floral 3" squares. Layer a marked square on an orange check or orange B square, right sides together. Sew ¼" from both sides of the drawn line. Cut the unit apart on the marked line. Make eight matching half-square-triangle units and trim them to 2½" square, including seam allowances. Repeat to make four sets of eight matching units.

Make 4 sets of 8 matching units.

2 Join a cream floral and orange check or orange B 1½" × 2½" piece to make a side unit

measuring 2½" square, including seam allowances. Make four sets of eight matching units.

Make 4 sets of 8 matching side units, 2½" × 2½".

3 Lay out four matching half-square-triangle units, four matching side units, and one cream floral 2½" square in three rows, rotating the units as shown. Sew all the pieces into rows and then join the rows. Make eight Churn Dash blocks measuring 6½" square, including seam allowances.

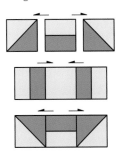 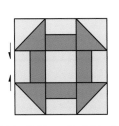

Make 8 Churn Dash blocks, 6½" × 6½".

4 Join two cream floral 2½" squares and one green A or B square to make a strip unit. Make eight units measuring 2½" × 6½", including seam allowances.

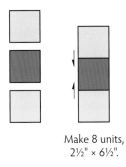

Make 8 units, 2½" × 6½".

5 Join four cream floral 4" × 6½" pieces, two different step 4 units, and a Churn Dash block to make a side border measuring 6½" × 24½", including seam allowances. Make two. Make two more borders in the same way, adding a Churn Dash block to each

Pat Sloan's Holiday Hoopla

end. The top and bottom borders should measure 6½" × 36½", including seam allowances.

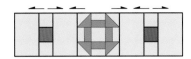

Make 2 side borders, 6½" × 24½".

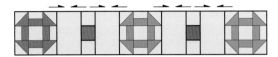

Make 2 top/bottom borders, 6½" × 36½".

Assembling the Quilt Top

1 Sew the green B 2" × 21½" strips to the top and bottom of the Pumpkin block. Sew the green B 2" × 24½" strips to the left and right sides. The quilt top should measure 24½" square, including seam allowances.

2 Sew the shorter Churn Dash borders to the left and right sides of the quilt top. Sew the longer Churn Dash borders to the top and bottom

edges. The quilt top should measure 36½" square, including seam allowances.

3 Sew the green B 2" × 36½" strips to the top and bottom edges. Sew the green B 2" × 39½" strips to the left and right sides. The quilt top should measure 39½" square.

Finishing the Quilt

For more details on any finishing steps, visit ShopMartingale.com/HowtoQuilt for free downloadable information.

1 Layer the quilt top with batting and backing; baste the layers together.

2 Quilt by hand or machine. The quilt shown is machine quilted with an allover pattern of leaves and swirls.

3 Use the orange check 2¼"-wide strips to make double-fold binding. Attach the binding to the quilt.

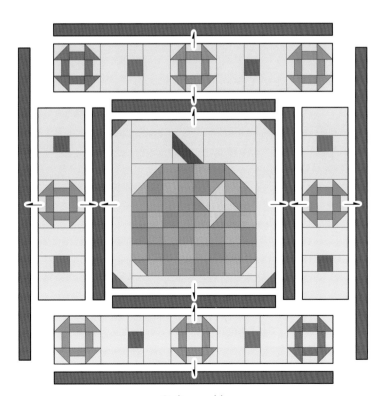

Quilt assembly

Thankful

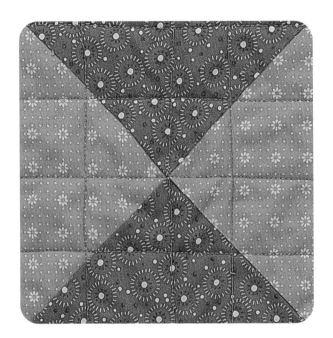

My favorite holiday is Thanksgiving Day, and this fall-colored Tree of Life quilt can be the perfect backdrop for your gatherings. Enjoy celebrating a day for being with family and friends to give thanks. This peaceful holiday holds lots of traditions for many of us, from certain foods to special serving dishes that we only use for Thanksgiving Day. Every seven years, this holiday is also my birthday. On those years I have both pie and birthday cake!

Materials

Yardage is based on 42"-wide fabric.

- ⅝ yard of taupe linen for Tree blocks
- 9 squares, 7" × 7" *each*, of assorted orange, gold, brown, and rust (collectively referred to as "orange") prints for Tree blocks
- 7" × 7" square of brown check for Tree blocks
- ⅓ yard of brown dot for Tree blocks
- 5" × 10" piece of red dot for center block
- 5" × 10" piece of orange dot for center block
- 1⅛ yards of green floral for center block, setting triangles, and binding
- 1⅛ yards of fabric for backing
- 39" × 39" piece of batting

Cutting

All measurements include ¼" seam allowances.

From the taupe linen, cut:
1 strip, 5" × 42"; crosscut into:
    2 squares, 5" × 5"
    12 squares, 2½" × 2½"
1 strip, 4½" × 42"; crosscut into 8 squares, 4½" × 4½"
3 strips, 3" × 42"; crosscut into 32 squares, 3" × 3"

From *each* of the assorted orange prints, cut:
4 squares, 3" × 3" (36 total; 4 will be extra)

Continued on page 84

Fun Days to Celebrate in November

November 3: *National Sandwich Day*

November 9: *Go to an Art Museum Day*

Third Monday in November: *Odd Socks Day*

November 17: *National Homemade Bread Day*

November 30: *National Mason Jar Day*

Continued from page 83

From the brown check, cut:

4 squares, 2½" × 2½"

From the brown dot, cut:

1 strip, 5" × 42"; crosscut into:

    2 squares, 5" × 5"

    4 squares, 4½" × 4½"

1 strip, 3" × 42"; crosscut into 8 squares, 3" × 3"

From the red dot, cut:

2 squares, 4½" × 4½"

From the orange dot, cut:

2 squares, 4½" × 4½"

From the green floral, cut:

1 strip, 18½" × 42"; crosscut into:

    1 square, 18½" × 18½"; cut the squares into

      quarters diagonally to yield 4 side triangles

    2 squares, 9½" × 9½"; cut the squares in half

      diagonally to yield 4 corner triangles

1 strip, 6½" × 42"; crosscut into 4 squares, 6½" × 6½"

4 strips, 2¼" × 42"

Making the Tree Blocks

Press seam allowances in the directions indicated by the arrows.

1 Draw a diagonal line from corner to corner on the wrong side of the taupe 3" squares. Layer a marked square on an orange 3" square, right sides together. Sew ¼" from both sides of the drawn line. Cut the unit apart on the marked line. Make 64 half-square-triangle units and trim them to 2½" square, including seam allowances.

Make 64 units.

2 Lay out nine half-square-triangle units, two taupe 2½" squares, and one brown check square in two rows, noting the direction of the triangles. Sew all the pieces into rows and then join the rows. Make four A units measuring 4½" × 12½", including seam allowances.

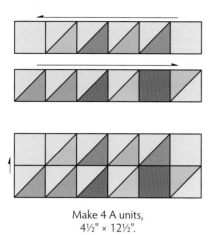

Make 4 A units,
4½" × 12½".

3 Lay out seven half-square-triangle units and one taupe 2½" square in two rows, noting the direction of the triangles. Sew all the pieces into rows and then join the rows. Make four B units measuring 4½" × 8½", including seam allowances.

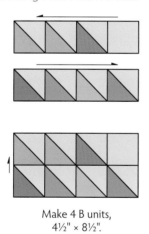

Make 4 B units,
4½" × 8½".

4 Draw a diagonal line from corner to corner on the wrong side of the brown dot 3" squares. Place a marked square on one corner of a taupe 4½" square. Sew on the marked line. Trim the excess

corner fabric ¼" from the stitched line. Make eight C units measuring 4½" square, including seam allowances.

Make 8 C units,
4½" × 4½".

5 Draw a diagonal line from corner to corner on the wrong side of the taupe 5" squares. Layer a marked square on a brown dot 5" square, right sides together. Sew ¼" from both sides of the drawn line. Cut the unit apart on the marked line. Make four half-square-triangle units and trim them to 4½" square, including seam allowances.

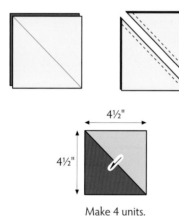

Make 4 units.

6 Lay out two C units, one brown dot 4½" square, and one half-square-triangle unit from step 5 in two rows. Sew all the pieces into rows and then join the rows to make a trunk unit. Make four units measuring 8½" square, including seam allowances.

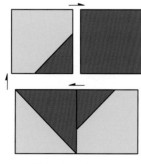

Make 4 trunk units,
8½" × 8½".

7 Sew a B unit to the right side of a trunk unit. Sew an A unit to the top edge to make a Tree block. Make four blocks measuring 12½" square, including seam allowances.

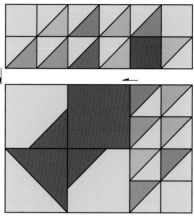

Make 4 tree blocks,
12½" × 12½".

Making the Center Block

1 Draw a diagonal line from corner to corner on the wrong side of the red and orange dot 4½" squares. Place a marked square on one corner of a green 6½" square. Sew on the marked line. Trim the excess corner fabric ¼" from the stitched line. Make two red and two orange dot units measuring 6½" square, including seam allowances.

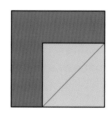 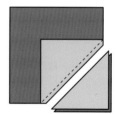

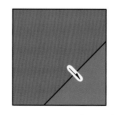 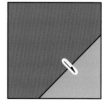

Make 2 of each unit,
6½" × 6½".

2 Lay out the units in two rows, rotating them so the red and orange triangles are in the center and like colors are diagonally opposite one another. Sew the units into rows and then join the rows to make a center block measuring 12½" square, including seam allowances.

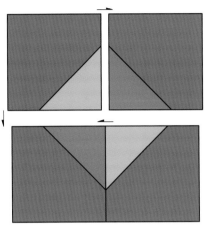

Make 1 center block,
12½" × 12½".

Assembling the Quilt Top

Referring to the quilt assembly diagram below, arrange and sew the Tree and center blocks in diagonal rows, adding the side triangles to the ends of the rows. Join the rows, adding the corner triangles last. The quilt top should measure 34½" square.

Finishing the Quilt

For more details on any finishing steps, visit ShopMartingale.com/HowtoQuilt for free downloadable information.

1 Layer the quilt top with batting and backing; baste the layers together.

2 Quilt by hand or machine. The quilt shown is machine quilted in a crosshatch pattern, using the size of the triangles in the trees as the guidelines for the spacing of the grid.

3 Use the green floral 2¼"-wide strips to make double-fold binding. Attach the binding to the quilt.

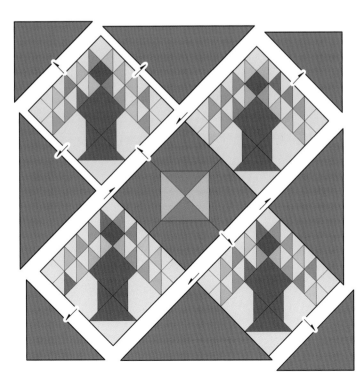

Quilt assembly

Welcome In

FINISHED QUILT: 34½" × 34½" • **FINISHED BLOCK: 18" × 18"**

Creating a welcoming home is a must-do for me at the holidays. And evergreens play a big role for both their style and scent. From trees to wreaths, evergreens make December festive. I love seeing evergreen swags on porches with big red bows and also evergreens in the yard decorated with white lights. My mother-in-law always bought the largest evergreen wreath she could find, with a great big bow. It was so gorgeous. This wreath is for you, Madge!

Materials

Yardage is based on 42"-wide fabric. Fat eighths measure 9" × 21".

- ¼ yard of gold print for Wreath block
- ½ yard of green print for Wreath block and border 3
- ⅞ yard of white print for Wreath block and borders
- 4" × 9" piece of red stripe for bow
- 1 yard of red floral for bow, borders, and binding
- 1 fat eighth of red print for ribbon
- 1⅛ yards of fabric for backing
- 39" × 39" piece of batting

Cutting

All measurements include ¼" seam allowances. As you cut, label the pieces as indicated for easy assembly.

From the gold print, cut:
2 strips, 3" × 42"; crosscut into:
    16 squares, 3" × 3"
    8 squares, 2½" × 2½"

Continued on page 90

Fun Days to Celebrate in December

December 4: *National Cookie Day*

Third Friday in December: *National Ugly Sweater Day*

December 19: *Look for an Evergreen Day*

December 21: *National Crossword Puzzle Day*

December 28: *National Call a Friend Day*

December 30: *National Bacon Day*

Continued from page 89

From the green print, cut:

2 strips, 3" × 42"; crosscut into:
- 18 squares, 3" × 3"
- 2 strips, 2" × 6½"
- 2 pieces, 2" × 3½"

1 strip, 2½" × 42"; crosscut into 16 squares, 2½" × 2½"

4 strips, 1½" × 42"; crosscut into:
- 2 strips, 1½" × 30½"
- 2 strips, 1½" × 28½"
- 4 squares, 1½" × 1½"

From the white print, cut:

1 strip, 3½" × 42"; crosscut into:
- 1 square, 3½" × 3½" (D)
- 4 squares, 3" × 3" (A)

5 strips, 2½" × 42"; crosscut into:
- 4 pieces, 2½" × 6½" (C)
- 4 pieces, 2½" × 4½" (B)
- 48 squares, 2½" × 2½" (P)
- 2 pieces, 1¼" × 2½" (F)

2 strips, 2" × 42"; crosscut into:
- 2 strips, 2" × 24½" (O)
- 1 square, 2" × 2" (K)

4 strips, 1½" × 42"; crosscut into:
- 2 strips, 1½" × 21½" (N)
- 2 strips, 1½" × 17½" (M)
- 2 strips, 1½" × 7" (G)
- 2 strips, 1½" × 6½" (L)
- 2 pieces, 1½" × 4" (J)
- 2 pieces, 1½" × 3½" (H)
- 2 pieces, 1½" × 2½" (I)
- 16 squares, 1½" × 1½" (E)

From the red stripe, cut:

2 pieces, 3½" × 4"

From the red floral, cut:

7 strips, 2½" × 42"; crosscut into:
- 2 strips, 2½" × 34½"
- 2 strips, 2½" × 30½"
- 24 pieces, 2½" × 4½"
- 1 piece, 2" × 2½"

4 strips, 2¼" × 42"

2 squares, 3" × 3"

From the red print, cut:

2 strips, 1½" × 21"; crosscut into:
- 4 pieces, 1½" × 4½"
- 2 pieces, 1½" × 4"
- 2 pieces, 1½" × 2½"
- 4 squares, 1½" × 1½"

1 square, 2" × 2"

Making the Wreath Block

Press seam allowances in the directions indicated by the arrows.

1 Draw a diagonal line from corner to corner on the wrong side of the gold 3" squares. Layer a marked square on a green 3" square, right sides together. Sew ¼" from both sides of the drawn line. Cut the unit apart on the marked line. Make 32 gold/green half-square-triangle units and trim them to 2½" square, including seam allowances.

2½"
2½"

Make 32 units.

2 Draw a diagonal line from corner to corner on the wrong side of two white A squares. Repeat step 1 using the marked squares and the remaining green squares to make four white/green triangle units and trim them to 2½" square, including seam allowances.

2½"
2½"

Make 4 units.

3 Lay out six gold/green half-square-triangle units, two green 2½" squares, and one gold 2½" square in three rows, rotating the units as shown. Sew the units into rows and then join the rows. Make four star units measuring 6½" square, including seam allowances.

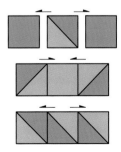 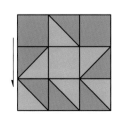

Make 4 star units,
6½" × 6½".

4 Draw a diagonal line from corner to corner on the wrong side of eight green 2½" squares. Place a marked square on one end of a white B, right sides together. Sew on the marked line. Trim the excess corner fabric ¼" from the stitched line. Make four units measuring 2½" × 4½", including seam allowances.

Make 4 units,
2½" × 4½".

5 Place a marked green 2½" square on one end of a white C, right sides together. Sew on the marked line. Trim the excess corner fabric ¼" from the stitched line. Make four units measuring 2½" × 6½", including seam allowances.

Make 4 units,
2½" × 6½".

6 Lay out one unit each from steps 4 and 5, one white/green half-square-triangle unit, two gold/green half-square-triangle units, and one gold 2½" square in three rows, noting the orientation of the triangle units. Sew all the pieces into rows and then join the rows. Make four corner units measuring 6½" square, including seam allowances.

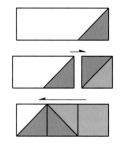 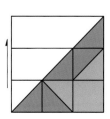

Make 4 corner units,
6½" × 6½".

7 Draw a diagonal line from corner to corner on the wrong side of the green 1½" squares. Place marked squares on the corners of a white D. Sew on the marked lines. Trim the excess corner fabric ¼" from the stitched lines.

Make 1 unit,
3½" × 3½".

8 Sew green 2" × 3½" pieces to the top and bottom of the unit from step 7. Sew green 2" × 6½" strips to the left and right sides to make a center unit measuring 6½" square.

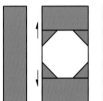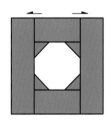

Make 1 center unit,
6½" × 6½".

9 Lay out the corner units, star units, and center unit in three rows to form a wreath. Sew the units into rows and then join the rows to make a Wreath block measuring 18½" square.

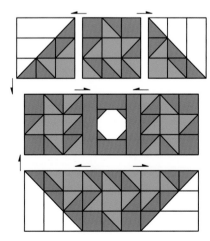

Make 1 Wreath block, 18½" × 18½".

Adding the Bow and Ribbon Borders

1 Draw a diagonal line from corner to corner on the wrong side of 14 white E squares. Place marked squares on two corners of a red stripe piece, noting the direction of the marked lines. Sew on the marked lines. Trim the excess corner fabric ¼" from the stitched lines. Make two bow units measuring 3½" × 4", including seam allowances.

Make 2 units,
3½" × 4".

2 Sew white F pieces to the long edges of the red floral 2" × 2½" piece to make the bow knot, which should measure 2½" × 3½", including seam allowances.

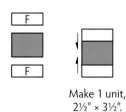

Make 1 unit,
2½" × 3½".

3 Place a marked E from step 1 on one end of a red print 1½" × 4" piece, right sides together. Sew on the marked line. Trim the excess corner fabric ¼" from the stitched line. Make one and one mirror-image unit measuring 1½" × 4", including seam allowances.

Make 1 of each unit,
1½" × 4".

Pat Sloan's Holiday Hoopla

4 Lay out one each of white G, H, I, and J, one unit from step 3, and one 1½" red print square in three rows as shown. Sew the pieces into rows and then join the rows to make a ribbon unit measuring 3½" × 7", including seam allowances. Repeat using the mirror-image unit from step 3 to make a mirror-image ribbon unit.

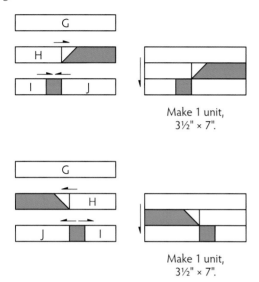

Make 1 unit,
3½" × 7".

Make 1 unit,
3½" × 7".

5 Join the units from step 4 and the bow units from steps 1 and 2 to make the top border, which should measure 3½" × 22½", including seam allowances.

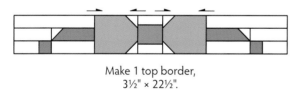

Make 1 top border,
3½" × 22½".

6 Draw a diagonal line from corner to corner on the wrong side of the white K square. Layer the marked square on a red print 2" square, right sides together. Sew ¼" from both sides of the drawn line. Cut the unit apart on the marked line. Make two half-square-triangle units and trim them to 1½" square, including seam allowances.

1½"
1½"
Make 2 units.

7 Place a marked E from step 1 on one end of a red print 1½" × 2½" piece, right sides together. Repeat step 3 to sew and trim. Make one and one mirror-image unit measuring 1½" × 2½", including seam allowances. In the same way, use marked squares and the red print 1½" × 4½" pieces to make the units indicated, noting the angle of the white pieces.

Make 1 of each unit,
1½" × 2½".

Make 1 of each unit,
1½" × 4½".

Make 1 of each unit,
1½" × 4½".

8 Lay out one red print 1½" square, one white M, one white E, one white L, one half-square-triangle unit, and one of each unit from step 7 in two rows as shown on page 94. Sew the pieces into rows

and then join the rows to make a left side border measuring 2½" × 18½", including seam allowances. Repeat to make the right side border, using the mirror-image units from step 7.

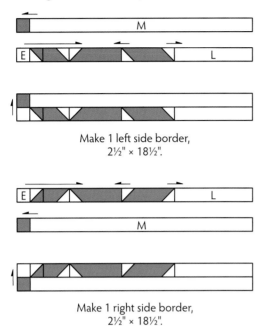

Make 1 left side border,
2½" × 18½".

Make 1 right side border,
2½" × 18½".

9 Sew the borders from step 8 to the left and right sides of the Wreath block. Sew the border from step 5 to the top edge. The quilt top should measure 21½" × 22½", including seam allowances. Sew the white N strip to the left and right sides of the quilt top. Sew the white O strip to the top and bottom edges. The quilt top should measure 24½" square, including seam allowances.

Making the Flying-Geese Borders

1 Draw a diagonal line from corner to corner on the wrong side of the white P squares. Place a marked square on one end of a red floral 2½" × 4½" piece, right sides together. Sew on the marked line. Trim the excess corner fabric ¼" from the stitched line. Place a marked square on the opposite end

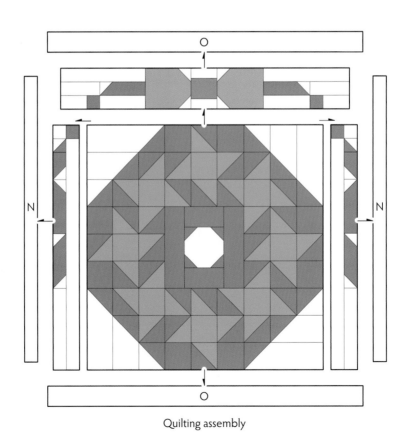

Quilting assembly

Pat Sloan's Holiday Hoopla

of the red piece. Sew and trim as before. Make 24 flying-geese units measuring 2½" × 4½".

Make 24 units,
2½" × 4½".

2 Draw a diagonal line from corner to corner on the wrong side of two white A squares. Layer a marked square on a red floral square, right sides together. Sew ¼" from both sides of the drawn line. Cut the unit apart on the marked line. Make four half-square-triangle units and trim them to 2½" square, including seam allowances.

Make 4 units.

3 Join five flying-geese units and two triangle units to make a side border measuring 2½" × 24½", including seam allowances. Make two. Join seven flying-geese units to make the top border. Repeat to make the bottom border. The top and bottom borders should measure 2½" × 28½", including seam allowances.

Make 2 side borders, 2½" × 24½".

Make 2 top/bottom borders, 2½" × 28½".

Adding the Borders

1 Referring to the quilt assembly diagram above right, sew the shorter flying-geese borders to the left and right sides of the quilt top. Sew the

longer flying-geese borders to the top and bottom edges. The quilt top should measure 28½" square, including seam allowances.

2 Sew the green 1½" × 28½" strips to the left and right sides of the quilt top. Sew the green 1½" × 30½" strips to the top and bottom edges. The quilt top should measure 30½" square, including seam allowances.

3 Sew the red floral 2½" × 30½" strips to the left and right sides of the quilt top. Sew the red floral 2½" × 34½" strips to the top and bottom edges. The quilt top should measure 34½" square.

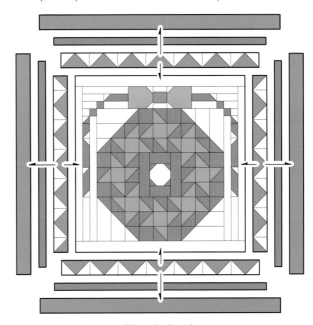

Adding the borders

Finishing the Quilt

For more details on any finishing steps, visit ShopMartingale.com/HowtoQuilt for free downloadable information.

1 Layer the quilt top with batting and backing; baste the layers together.

2 Quilt by hand or machine. The quilt shown is machine quilted with an allover swirl design.

3 Use the red floral 2¼"-wide strips to make double-fold binding. Attach the binding to the quilt.

Acknowledgments

A huge thank-you goes to my long-arm quilters Judy Clark, Cindy Dickinson, and Dennis Dickinson.

Another thank-you goes to my business partners—Aurifil (thread), Baby Lock (machines), OLFA (cutters), and Benartex (fabric).

All this could not be possible without my amazing editor, Nancy Mahoney; Martingale's Content Director, Karen Soltys; and the whole Martingale team.

About the Author

I'm a quilt designer, author, teacher, YouTuber, and fabric designer. My passion is to make quilting fun for everyone. I love to make quilts, share quilts, and talk about quilts. I host a very active, friendly, and exciting quilting community on Facebook called Quilt Along with Pat Sloan. I host lots of sew-alongs and challenges, and we have so much fun—please join us! Find me at PatSloan.com and sign up for my notices. I can't wait to chat with you!

What's your creative passion?
Find it at ShopMartingale.com
books • eBooks • ePatterns • blog • free projects
videos • tutorials • inspiration • giveaways

Martingale®
Create with Confidence